ENTREPRENEURSHIP
Unwrap the Genius in You

BY MARIETTE KUSSMAUL

KUDU

Entrepreneurship: Unwrap the Genius in You

by Mariette Kussmaul

Copyright © 2012 by Mariette Kussmaul

Published by Kudu Publishing

Trade Paperback ISBN: 978-1-9386240-0-1
eBook ISBN: 978-1-9386240-1-8

Available in Amazon Kindle, Apple iBooks and Barnes & Noble Nook formats.

Cover Design: Martijn van Tilborgh

DEDICATION
Why I Wrote This Book

I dedicate this book, Entrepreneurship: Unwrap the Genius in You, *to my father Neville Halberg, whom I'm extremely proud of, as the passion of entrepreneurship was deposited in me from childhood. Dad was an example of determination as he identified obstacles in Zambia and positioned himself from a platform of power to ensure we, his family, were always safe and encouraged us to embrace life's challenges. He lived, dreamed, and operated in the fullness and success of a true entrepreneur.*

Dad, thank you. You are a genius who never ceases to impress me. For that, I am forever grateful as your entrepreneurship is a living example of all things being possible and that we should never limit ourselves.

TABLE OF CONTENTS

FOREWORD

Inspired by a vision to have a new and richer world in front of her, Mariette has vivid pictures of what is inherently in her and what gifts are in each person. Her talent to discover, draw out, and develop the natural abilities in a person is an absolute gift. She truly has lived what she writes about.

In this book, Mariette has intuitive ideas along with practical application for every person from any walk of life anywhere they may find themselves. It is an absolute *must* read for every business-minded person. I am privileged to have been asked to write the foreword for this book. I, too, am a student of entrepreneurship.

Mariette has been an inspiration, major motivator, and mentor to me personally. She truly has helped uncover hidden talents in me propelling me forward in my own life and career. What a pleasure to be associated with Mariette and see her in action, living what she has written in her book. It is fabulous to know she actually practices, and has become successful with, what she teaches others.

Counting Mariette a friend is an absolute blessing! With her oh-so-encouraging, go-after-it attitude, I admire the accomplishments she makes through her actions on a daily basis. Her success is well deserved!

—SARAH A. LINDSTROM, ENTREPRENEUR

INTRODUCTION

I believe with everything in me, that as an entrepreneur myself, my purpose on this earth is to help you release the unwrapped genius in you.

Your gifting and talents will become prominent and obvious to you while reading this book. Only you can release your full potential, but I can alert your spirit (your heart) and guide you to be the signature entrepreneur you should be and will be!

It is time to stop procrastinating, making all kinds of excuses, and allow your passion to put pen to paper taking your idea to the next level. I challenge you to change the atmosphere around you and grasp this opportunity to define your vision, learn the rules, build your team, mobilize the essential resources, make a commitment, and become the unstoppable you.

You will notice in this book I have three areas of importance after each chapter:

- Red Flag: the most common problem experienced in that chapter
- Words of wisdom given from the Book of Proverbs
- Journal page for a self-evaluation, take-action

tools, and thoughts
- Ask and Answer section to prompt your mind to think out of the box.

Entrepreneurs are very unique and special people as they are:

- ✓ Self-driven
- ✓ Opportunists
- ✓ Problem solvers
- ✓ Creative thinkers*
- ✓ Calculated risk takers
- ✓ Extrovert personality characteristics
- ✓ Propelled by excellence

*Creative being the mindset of a millionaire

They are proactive, forward thinkers and do not understand the misfortune of procrastination. I am certain you have identified yourself in this powerful description!

You are at the top of the entrepreneurial process. As you are unique, so is your personal signature idea. No one else can better prepare the plan and strategize your project than you. You will make things happen, and that is what excites you.

In the book, I have introduced the concept of how the entrepreneurial traits of my father's character and lifestyle influenced me from childhood, while living in Zambia and South Africa, and during my self-development as a successful entrepreneur. I trust you will enjoy the analogies and stories as much as I loved living them.

This book, *Entrepreneurship: Unwrap the Genius in You*, will guide you step-by-step, day-by-day to stay passionate and motivated. You will discover the planner in you, the focused strategist, and, ultimately, the confident billionaire. How is that for a deal?

Chapter I

WORK IN YOUR GENIUS

My father was a genius, and I like to think he was my genius. Dad was always dealing with mechanical things in whatever business he started. I was recently recounting to myself some of the things he had been involved with during his life: diamond drilling machines, auto dealerships, aircraft dealerships, auto body shops, car racing circuits in Africa, the President's Aircraft Race, and constructing buildings while being an example to family and friends. He was a man with a zest for life.

Dad seldom used a calculator when doing any of the intricate things he accomplished in his busy days. He would invent machines to build auto pistons for his race cars, tally the daily receipts, and do a multitude of other things—promptly calculating in his head without fail.

I could always tell when Dad had seen something in his mind's eye. He had a certain look about him when he "saw" a new idea. I could almost hear his mind shifting gears as he was structuring the business or assembling the new machine in his mind. It was in one of these moments that Dad's genius was awakened in me for greater things in my life.

He was a perfect fit in the world of business. It was where his greatest gifting lay, and he nurtured his gifting and expanded, always reaching out for the next challenge. When all he had created in Zambia was repossessed by the government, he went to South Africa and recreated a new world of business.

At the tender age of around twelve, Dad began to develop my gifting and guided me into his world of entrepreneurship. These were exciting years for me as he began to assemble me as if he were constructing one of his many inventions. It was a mixture of fun and hard work. I can never thank him enough as I am convinced he did not even know what he was doing.

As I experienced life in the business world, I made a decision to bring tremendous focus into my life, and I started preparing and training for running and cycling ultra-marathons. I had to discipline myself, and through a structured lifestyle, I not only developed endurance within myself, but I acquired tremendous focus for whatever I set my mind to accomplish. I now work in my core giftings—they are *my genius!*

You become unstoppable as you work in your genius—you are a genius! I researched the word *genius,* and this is what I found:

> Genius—natural ability or capacity; an exceptional natural capacity of intellect and creative power (*Webster's College Dictionary*)

Once you truly accept what is inside of you and tap into that resource, the sky is no limitation for you. You can do anything you want when you work from a position of power and strength and in your genius. You need to be operating in your gifting—your genius—because your gifting will set the boundaries as to what you accept and reject. You will naturally surround yourself with like-minded people.

A good example of what I am saying is that of triathletes. They could quite easily talk about their sport day in and day out with passion, knowledge, and extraordinary wisdom. Why does this happen? It's so because their natural abilities, strengths, efforts, and understanding of other triathletes complements and encourages their conversations and beliefs.

These triathletes have recognized opportunities or ideas that fit their personal objectives, skills, risk tolerances, and passions. (Triathletes embody less than one percent of the world population.)

Opportunities or entrepreneurial ideas have inherent characteristics that enable them to be converted into positive, sustainable cash-flow machines in the right hands and under the right conditions. To maximize your capacity for output, you need to train your conscious mind to be in the present—in the moment—focused and determined to succeed. Donald Trump made this statement: "My policy is to learn from the past, focus on the present, and dream about the future." These are wise words for an entrepreneur.

Do you really know what pushes your buttons? What turns you on, and what really gets your goat? Deep inside of you there is a person, a place, an idea which just needs you to recognize it, nurture it, cultivate it, and work it by preparing and positioning yourself for overflow and abundance. Your cash machine needs you to pull the handle now! May I suggest you do a SWOT analysis? Especially if you are not sure and need confirmation of what you think of yourself and where your strengths and weaknesses lie, you should use this tool. SWOT stands for:

S—strengths
W—weaknesses
O—opportunities
T—threats

Complete the SWOT analysis in your journal at the end of this chapter. This tool will help bring clarity to your strengths and weaknesses. It will help you realize what opportunities you have in the hat and which threats may be keeping you from running with your ideas. This is a powerful and interesting exercise as it highlights areas of concern, which you should eliminate, and permits you to operate from a position of power while working in your season of opportunities. The strength of your dreams relies a whole lot on the outcome of your SWOT analysis.

Why SWOT? What makes SWOT particularly powerful is that, with a little thought, it can help you uncover opportunities that you are well placed to exploit. And by understanding the weaknesses of your business, you can manage and eliminate threats that would otherwise catch you unaware. By looking at yourself and your competitors using the SWOT analysis, you can start to craft a strategy that helps you distinguish yourself and your ideas from your competitors so that you can compete successfully as an entrepreneur and in the market place:

Strengths:

- What do you do better than anyone else?
- What unique or low-cost resources can you draw upon that others cannot?

Weaknesses:

- What should you avoid?
- What are people in your market likely to see as weaknesses?

Opportunities:

- What unique opportunities can you spot related to your strengths?

Threats:

- Could any of your weaknesses seriously threaten your business?
- What business obstacles do you face?

By completing the SWOT exercise, you have conquered the brain freeze that often plagues us in business situations. You know who you are; you have worked at who you want to be and know what is expected as an entrepreneur. Now you can work on developing your idea. Remember that clarity and simplicity are vital keys of business. This SWOT analysis can be applied to any situation in your business: the viability of your idea, the employment of managers and staff, financial implications, and so forth.

You have now empowered yourself, and I am certain you are extremely excited about building and empowering your ideas. Empowering a business idea is one of the most exciting sections of preparing a business plan as your right brain of creativity is engaged in this process big time!

Your idea must fit you like your best pair of shoes—a perfect fit! Finding the perfect fit is like separating the diamonds from the coals. Your diamond idea, as with your best pair of shoes, must complement what you are wearing and what statement you wish it to make. During a business presentation, you would not wear your running shoes, would you? Therefore, your diamond idea must present a concept of opportunities in the business mix and who you are!

Most entrepreneurs assume that their creative ideas can be commercialized readily into profitable businesses. Oh, no. This is not so! An idea is just that—an idea—and if it does not hold opportunities for your business, not one dollar should be spent on it. It is a nonstarter and will drain you of all your funding. However, if you are sure that you have an opportunity, there will be no limitations to your success.

The challenges for you are to become aware and constantly search our beautiful environment for new, different, better, purposeful, and innovative ideas that can be attached to a handful of opportunities to fulfill a particular need for generations and, as a bonus, build a cash flow. In fact, any idea that can actually become a positive, sustainable cash machine can become an opportunity.

Opportunities need to be screened and filtered to eliminate the ones that are a waste of time and do not fit the genius in you! Here are some filtering questions you may ask about the opportunity presenting itself:

> Does your product or service fulfill needs?
>
> Is the market large and growing?
>
> Is there a potential for repeat sales?
>
> Do you require large amounts of capital for your product or service?
>
> Do you and your team possess the necessary entrepreneurial traits and industry knowledge and skills?
>
> Will your business be a low-cost producer, the most differentiated producer, or both?
>
> Have you identified potential flaws and not just opportunities?

Look inside yourself; there is a ready template to test your comfort level when you think about your own business. Good things rarely come to entrepreneurs who wait patiently. If your deep-centered goal in life is to start and grow your own successful business, it just won't happen unless you are proactive to the extreme. Success comes to those who are doing—not just thinking and talking.

Summary

You have learned much in this first chapter. You've read the SWOT analysis and have begun to identify the true you. You've asked yourself filtering questions about your idea and opportunities. You've learned to evaluate the difference between ideas and ideas that become opportunities to generate the flow and income of a successful business. More than just knowing your strengths, weaknesses, and the opportunities and threats that lie ahead, write them in the journal section. You are a doer developing wisdom.

Red Flag

Take time to recognize that your idea (with its opportunities) is the right mix between business potential and your ability to reach that potential, given your position, core competence, strengths, weaknesses, and resources.

Words of Wisdom

> A man's gift makes room for him and brings him before great men.
>
> —PROVERBS 18:16

Journal

1.) Complete the SWOT.

2.) Write your skills, resources, ideas, and experiences.

Ask and Answer

Do I have or could I gather what is marketable?

Strengths	Weaknesses

My Skills:

_____

_____

My Resources:

_____

_____

My Ideas:

_____

_____

My Experiences:

_____

_____

Do I have something marketable?

Explain: _____

_____

Chapter 2

PASSION-EXCELLING SUCCESS

My father was an excellent example to me. He showed passion and commitment in everything he endeavored. It was no problem for him to sacrifice sleep, 3 or 4 hours a night, to meet his deadlines. At about the age of twenty, he lost one of his eyes in an accident. Despite this adversity, Dad was unstoppable in anything he did.

It was this spirit of determination and tenacity to see each job through to completion that led him into the world of business. He was very successful in whatever he started. I was born into this atmosphere and was captivated by its vibrancy. At one point, Dad was the Piper Aircraft distributor for Central Africa. He also owned and operated a farm, a fuel station, and auto dealerships. He was also known for having the most popular auto repair staff in Zambia and South Africa.

This was the time of Zambia's nationalization, and the government was restricting many businesses and simply taking over many other larger operations such as copper mines and electric companies. This was a time of internal trouble, and all the tribes were involved as they fought for control. He knew our family's days in Zambia were numbered and began to plan for our ultimate departure.

My siblings and I were sent to a South African boarding school and had about four months at home each year with our parents and relatives. At the age of twelve, I started spending some school holidays working with my dad. I did some bookwork, small administration jobs, and design checklists for the cars repaired prior to their release to the customers. Blessed to be in a position of observation, I had found my niche in life and would continue to develop this area.

We traveled with Dad across Africa in his aircraft, expanding his businesses into other countries. I gained so much wisdom and knowledge watching him in action with other businesspeople. He was very skilled in his negotiating with others during business proceedings, and I learned much as I noted the transactions.

My father always attracted people no matter where he was during his workday or after hours and on the weekend at the auto races. He drove his special Formula Ford race car, which he built himself. Dad was known by his friends and family as a genius in everything he did.

Where do I get my business knowledge and passion? I got it directly from my father, and I am thrilled to be able to pass this amazing heritage on to you.

Passion is adrenaline. It is a natural chemical in our bodies that is frequently referred to as the "happy drug" that accelerates everything in us: mood, blood pressure, nervous system, release of serotonin, outlook on life, and positive thinking. It makes us want to run rather than walk. What a position of power and excellence to operate from, driven by sheer unity in body, mind, and soul!

As entrepreneurs, it is possible that we function at this level of passion 85 percent of our day. We are excited by an idea, conversation about business, or opportunity knocking, and we have the ability to drift into overdrive. Our minds never cease to function as we continuously identify possibilities, solve problems, work plans, strategize moves, and sense winning breakthroughs. Passion unlocks your potential. It gives you permission to work in your genius!

It is said that only 44 percent of new businesses make it to their fourth year. If all entrepreneurs followed their own passions, this statistic would be far higher. But sad to say, far too often aspiring entrepreneurs and even college students, instead of following their hearts, follow the crowd and end up terribly disappointed.

No one can teach you the intangible quality that separates the average businessperson from an inspiring communicator, leader, and visionary. All are obsessed with what they do! All successful entrepreneurs are passionate about their products, services, companies, or causes. Instead of doing what others told them, they do what they feel in their guts, in their innermost beings, and make successful businesses out of the things that consume their thoughts.

I believe you do not find your true passion—it finds you! Passions are irresistible. If you're paying attention to your life, the things you are passionate about just won't leave you alone. They are the ideas, hopes, pictures in your mind, possibilities to which your mind naturally gravitates, and things on which you would focus your time and attention. Doing them feels natural and right. I have yet to meet a person with a meaningful life who has not based it on extraordinary passion.

Starting a business is laden with obstacles and setbacks, but with passion and listening to that inner voice, failure is never an option. Entrepreneurs should be fully aware of obstacles but also understand the process of turning an obsession into a brilliant idea, product, or service that meets a customer's need. That customer must be passionate about your product too. Passion must drive your every thought as an entrepreneur.

Let us take a look at the unstoppable you for a moment or two. What does it mean to be unstoppable? *Webster's Dictionary* says is means "free from any obstacles." Or in other words, nothing is impossible. Does this sound like you? Sure, there are split seconds when we doubt, but we quickly, ingeniously become problem solvers and passionately pick ourselves up and run with the tasks ahead of us. We are unstoppable.

Unstoppable entrepreneurs search for answers, knowledge, and wisdom from books, the Internet, family, and friends. They are calculated risk takers, not calculated fools. They stop at nothing until they have all the facts and figures to make the correct and wisest decisions that will lead to success and rewards. When a little boy dresses in his Batman suit, he instantly takes on the character of a genius.

Who are your heroes, and what is it about them that attracts you? I am certain you have recognized all the positive character traits in them, and that is good! However, it is not sufficient to recognize good qualities in others if we ourselves remain in places of disappointment and discouragement. So why do we do this? There are a few reasons for this, and I am going to list them so you can see which ones you recognize in yourself:

- You feel comfortable and do not want to be challenged.
- You feel unspectacular.
- You do not have confidence.
- There are certain lines you do not cross.
- You are fearful and have self-doubt.
- You do not have money.
- You feel like a fool and think your ideas are not worth anything.
- You fear success. (Oh, yes. There are people who do this.)
- You have never really recognized you have a dream.
- You do not know how to plan or start a business.

Do not feel alone, and please understand, it is just a feeling—it is not truth. Take your journal and list ten discouraging points. All you are required to do is change the discouragement into I CAN. This is your new mindset. You will notice, as you do this exercise, that the I CAN far outweighs your discouragement. You are becoming unstoppable and unwrapping the genius in you.

DISCOURAGED thoughts	I CAN thoughts

Here are some excellent entrepreneur characteristics you should take ownership of and develop in yourself. When you do so, passion will begin to rule your every thought.

- Open your eyes and dream.
- Search for your heart's desire.
- Get a clear picture of it in your mind—a vision.
- Write down your dream.
- Know that your spirit is designed for success—achievement.
- Can you feel the passion rising in your heart, mind, and body?
- Believe in the knowledge, skills, giftings and talents you have.
- Motivate and inspire yourself by removing false beliefs.
- Empower yourself, and set realistic goals for six months and one year.
- Know that you are a problem solver.

- Know that you can develop the skills you lack.
- Know that the sky is not the limit, and anything is possible.
- Know that passion keeps you enthusiastic, enhances energy, and gives you clarity.
- Develop time management, and know time is your friend.
- Unwrap the genius in you!

You are now ready to master your own destiny. Visualize your dream playing out on a screen in front of you. Get in the driver's seat, start up the engine, and drive into your destiny with passion.

What happens from this chapter forward is first a small, seemingly insignificant step, followed by more seemingly insignificant steps. Step-by-step, we are walking into the preparation period of identifying our personal strengths, product identities, and destinies of our businesses. Success is a decision. Congratulations! You have made that decision. Otherwise, you would have put this book down before you got to this page.

No one can live or plan your destiny for you except yourself, and it takes time to plan. Those who fail are the ones who fail to take the time to plan. You are not one of them since you have already started to plan. Did you know that there are real people who do extraordinary things with extraordinary success and are very happy doing these extraordinary assignments? It is said that 50 percent of the world's people are in very unhappy careers!

Your destiny is in the future. Your passion will drive and direct your thoughts. Your advantage, at present, is that you can highlight your planning with lessons learned from the past to ensure you do not repeat past mistakes. By planning, you will capitalize on what you have: your dreams, strengths, passions, talents, giftings, and visions. You also have the confidence and mentorship this book provides to guide you into your destiny.

Summary

You cannot step into your destiny if you are not prepared to take action and make changes in your life. You can talk it, pretend it, or write it, but if you do not change your mindset and develop passion in doing it and executing one step at a time, you will be in the same place ten years from now, and that is a fact. The best time to start is now and with oodles of passion.

Red Flag

Take time to ponder your dream and align it with your heart's desires to ensure passion will drive your every thought and action from now on.

Words of Wisdom

> In the end, people appreciate frankness more than flattery.
>
> —PROVERBS 28:23

Journal

1.) Write down your dream.

2.) Do the I CAN exercise.

Ask and Answer

Is my dream aligned with my passions, giftings, and talents? Can I step into my destiny with what I have?

My passion strategy:

_____

_____

Is my dream realistic?

_____

_____

Am I removing obstacles and unwrapping the genius in me?

_____

_____

Can I visualize my destiny—the end from the beginning?

_____

_____

Chapter 3

COMMUNICATION: THE POWER OF YOUR MOUTH AND EARS

For many it is difficult to understand what happens at the family level of a nation when its government is overthrown, and new and different systems of laws and dictates are forced upon the various peoples. In Zambia, where we three children were raised, the education system failed as the majority of qualified teachers fled the country. The financial system failed, and no funds were available.

My father had to adapt and bought an airplane to take us to boarding school in South Africa, two countries to the south. This put a tremendous strain on the whole family with Dad having to fly under extreme conditions through three different countries' airspace, and, at times, having to drive that distance when private aircraft were grounded by the Zambian government. As the oldest child, I had to take care of my younger brother and little sister. Here is a point I want you to see clearly: In times of crisis, in a nation falling apart, you must step up and make a way where there is no way. He did what had to be done to get an education for his children, and he got us to boarding school.

The rules of the boarding school were that only a set amount of money could be given to each child to spend at the shop for cokes, candy bars, and little things. Dad refused for us to be limited. He had raised us to work for, manage, and respect money; he refused to limit us while we were at school.

Our family's communication structure was disrupted, but life continued in fluid motion—just like a river. Sometimes the river is out of its banks and uncontrollable. Other times it is calm and smooth. This was a time of flood in our lives and in the country of Zambia. Legal, educational, and economic systems were swept away, and the infrastructure of the country fell apart as we watched.

What did we do? We did what we had to and changed our set pattern to overcome our situation. We were not prepared to live our lives in a country out of control as our father planned, worked, and reinvented our lives in a new country where the river was flowing calmly. Together, as a family unit, we reinvented our communication system, girded the loins of our minds, and did what we had to do.

How often have you walked away from a person or from a meeting and thought, "I should have said this. Or, they didn't get it, and I just did not get through to them"?

There could be many reasons for that, and in this chapter, we will address some of the common reasons and give suggestions on how to become an effective communicator and listener.

We each have our own styles of communication, but the most effective way to communicate is to adapt our styles to match the other person or situation. To be in a position to do this, you must first identify what your style is. We all have challenges in communicating with other people whose style of communication is different than ours. This is not unusual, but as entrepreneurs, we need to know our styles and understand the advantages we have in adapting to the other person's manner. I am not saying you must lose your identity as a communicator. Simply use and adapt your style to get the message across in the most effective way to achieve the best results in a win-win situation.

There are four styles of communication. You may find that during some situations you combine and express yourself in two of these modes. There are basically two types of people you will be dealing with: the receptive communicator and the purposed communicator. When you have identified which you are dealing with, you can then effectively adapt your style of communication and direct the end result for all to feel satisfied and happy.

Receptive Person

This type of person prefers to have an informal conversation before getting into actual business activities—my supportive husband, Ron, certainly matches this description. When you are in conversation with a receptive communicator, it is imperative to ask a few informal questions before getting into the subject matter.

Be aware. These people, indirect communicators, do not like to let people know too much about their personal lives. They are reserved in answering personal questions that will make them feel uneasy.

The speed of conversation with these individuals is slow and intentional; they find loud, fast, and excessively aggressive talk rather disturbing and can distance themselves from the conversation. They possess the quality to concentrate more on facts and figures, rather than on assumptions.

The Purposed Person

This is the direct talker, more clamorous and rapidly driven than indirect, receptive communicators. They take risks easily and are driven and self-assured. They are forward thinkers and ahead of the conversation in their minds as visualization and clarity come quickly to them.

When in communication with the intent/direct communicator, ensure you get to the point quickly as their minds are always busy strategizing. Be confident in what you say to them, provide solid instances of your achievements, and be alert when you talk to them.

You can release the genius in you by directing interaction and conversation. As an entrepreneur, it is inevitable that you understand the dispositions of the people you are dealing with. Identify their styles of communication and adapt yours to theirs. This is good customer relations!

Now let us address the four styles of communication. Take the time to identify yours clearly so you can know who you are and know how you can create a win-win situation!

The Controller

Controller communicators are extremely goal oriented, and their major motivation is getting things done. They love time lines and are able to take a project and run with it. At times, they won't even have a plan but just forge ahead and work it out as they go along. A controller has very little time for details, and giving them more details than necessary is confusing to them as it is not necessary.

Communicating Tips:

- Be efficient and business-like.
- Get to the point.
- Set and clarify goals and objectives.
- Only provide details if asked.
- Talk in terms of results not methods.

The Introducer

The introducer is the life and soul of a party and loves to have fun and laugh. They love people and love to talk, exhibiting a huge general knowledge base as they interact. They love to socialize and encourage others.

Introducers have an attractive personality. Their enthusiastic and expressive nature attracts others to them.

Communicating Tips:

- Leave plenty of time for talk and socializing.
- Ask them about their families and what they are up to.
- Be prepared to talk about yours as they are genuinely interested.
- If possible, let them experience what you are communicating.
- Talk in terms of people and stories—reality counts to them.
- Use lots of examples.

The Supporter

The supporter communicator typically has a low key personality and is calm, cool, and collected. They are patient, well balanced, and happily reconciled with life. They are content and steady workers who do not like to be involved in conflict. When there is conflict, they may call upon another to mediate the problem. They are good listeners and are motivated not to offend anyone.

Communicating Tips:

- Don't come on too strongly.
- Earn trust in small steps.
- Don't ask for big decisions—one step at a time is enough.
- Provide plenty of reassurance and security.
- Use testimonies as examples.

The Analyzer

Facts and figures are what counts with analyzers. They love to gather information and details and organize everything and everyone. They tend to be deep, thoughtful, analytical, serious, and purposeful. Their communication style includes a need for factual details; they sometimes hesitate to make decisions if they feel that they don't have enough facts.

They love lists, charts, graphs, and figures. They pay much attention to details and can seem to be pessimistic. They can be frugal and economical.

Communicating Tips:

- Make sure you are well prepared.
- Don't leave anything to chance.
- Do not exaggerate the facts—you will be found out.
- Have plenty of facts and figures.
- Be prepared for skepticism.
- Answer all their questions—do not avoid questions.
- Go relatively slowly to give them time to think and analyze.

I am certain you have recognized a little bit of you in each of the communicating styles. However, you do have a dominant manner about you, and that is considered to be your communication style.

May I take this opportunity to add the lost art of listening to this chapter? I am certain you will recognize communicating and listening go hand in hand. Everything we do requires communication. However, communication is a two way street: first, speaking and second, listening. Real communication and connection occur when the speaker and listener participate in the process.

Should you want to improve your listening skills, here are some thoughts on the subject that may make you more aware of the value of listening deliberately to the communicator. Be real, and watch your relationships grow.

Purpose to Listen Intentionally

Have you noticed when someone is speaking, you could be partially listening, while simultaneously planning the rest of your day? Paying attention is the cardinal rule for good listening. Hear the words, and let their meaning absorb into your consciousness.

Hear Them and Be Receptive

There is no problem with having goals for an interaction, but let them go while the other person is speaking, so you can hear what is being expressed. Balance your communication style with that of the communicator to sustain a harmonious relationship.

Listen With Empathy

Empathy is an imaginative process. It is the mindset that listens with the whole being and is not distracted by other thoughts. Empathy is a respectful understanding of what others are experiencing. True empathy is the ability to fully understand and accept others, complete with all their feelings, thoughts and opinions.

Repeat by Asking Questions

Focus on the communicator; notice his or her body language and tone of voice, and ask short relevant questions as you participate in the interaction.

It's Not About You

If you find yourself bored and distracted, reconnect with eye contact, uncross your arms, nod your head, and let the speaker know you are interested in what he or she is saying. It is hurtful when the "listener" is being dysfunctional.

Give the Speaker a Voice

Listen without formulating a quick response to the speaker. As listeners, we think about 600 words per minutes while the average speaking rate is 120 to 150 words per minute. This huge difference indicates how much can actually be misunderstood during a conversation.

Adapt Your Communication Style

To adapt your communication style to another's takes "listening," and that means you have to bring a fresh perspective to the relationship by intently using your efforts to listen. Let go of your need to be right or your ideas about what the person should be saying or doing; hear the person as if for the first time.

Listening is essential to fulfilling relationships—personal and business. Check if you just might exhibit any of the behaviors you find annoying.

Summary

Become aware of communication styles and your personal filters and triggers. Each of us is a product of upbringing, culture, life experiences, and anything and everything that makes us unique as human beings. One's uniqueness can sometimes be an obstacle to being an effective communicator and listener. Remain open and real when communicating, and withhold evaluation or judgment.

Red Flag

You think you are a good communicator and listener and do not have to make any adjustments. As an entrepreneur, there are always adjustments to make to be successful. It is all about your customers—not you.

Words of Wisdom

> Blessed are those who have a tender conscience,
> but the stubborn are headed for serious trouble.
>
> —PROVERBS 28:14

Journal

1.) Write down your communication style as you have identified it.

2.) Write down how you can adapt your style to create a win-win situation.

3.) Record three major character traits you have to give attention to before becoming a more effective entrepreneur and releasing the genius in you.

4.) Write down five benefits you will receive by becoming a better listener.

Ask and Answer

Do you believe your communication and listening styles could position you in the top ten best communicators in the world?

Chapter 4

THINK LIKE A BILLIONAIRE— IT'S ONLY A HABIT

t is amazing what circumstances can do for a person when those situations burst suddenly into your life. Many people get despondent and simply succumb to the situation. With others, the circumstances trigger hidden potential within them to survive and to conquer the problems of life; this is the mind-set of a billionaire.

When my innovative Dad was still a young boy, he would go to the farm next door, take the farmer's eggs, and sell them to contribute to the family's survival. Was it right? No! Was it required for the family to survive? Yes, so his young mind thought. This only lasted for a short while, for when my grandfather followed him one morning, the egg salesman was busted, put out of work, and things were made right. It was these situations that forced the development of hard work and courage to handle the challenges of life that were fostered early in my father's life.

I attended the University of Life as I traveled with my father across many countries of Africa, attended boarding school in South Africa, and accompanied him on business trips and holidays. I learned to speak three languages: English, Afrikaans, and Zulu. Later, as an adult, I traveled around the world. I highly recommend the University of Life. As you study the people around you and around the world, you gain tremendous perspective and insight into global business. You continuously hear the names of those countries' billionaires and take note of who and what they are.

I have always had the tenacity within myself to solve my own problems. We lived in northern Zambia when I was four and a half years old, and one day my parents were slightly late in picking me up from preschool. So, I innocently decided to walk home. The problem with this was that we were living on the dangerous border of Belgian Congo. Dad was drilling for diamonds in the deep bush, and the school was in a small town in Zambia. God had his hand upon my life even then. The police found me, and in a little while, my parents arrived to take me home. You must understand that Zambia was a very wild place with large numbers of lions, leopards, and baboons—not a gentle stroll in the park for a little girl. The Lord had a plan for my life.

As I have grown, I look back on my childhood as simpler times and difficult times, and I realize that pressure produces diamonds. Later on, I would have many businesses—one of which was a publishing company in South Africa. Here, I published a golf magazine for a South African named Ernie Else. I played many of the golf courses in South Africa and a few games with Ernie. An amazing entrepreneur himself, Ernie played and designed golf courses throughout the world. All things are possible if you believe and *think like a billionaire!*

Thinking like a billionaire is just a habit that can be developed. How do you think billionaires became billionaires? They set goals and worked with great passion and conviction toward achieving them.

In actuality, there really is no difference between you and a billionaire except your mindset.

A billion-dollar mindset is based upon the personal conviction that you determine your own destiny. What most people do not realize is that their experiences (the unwrapped geniuses in them) are reflections of their consciousness. The point is that you can train yourself and develop a habit; it's the process of success or failure to recognize opportunities or see difficulties, to know what you want and to go for it.

Your habits are the main contributing factors to becoming a billionaire or not! When Donald Trump was more than $900 million in debt, a reporter asked him this question: "What happened Mr. Trump?" Unlike most people who fail and blame the economy or say something about a real estate bubble that burst—even though that was the fact in Donald Trump's case—Mr. Trump admitted, "I took my eye off the ball. I stopped doing business the way I used to. So I got my eye back on the ball." He immediately propelled himself right back into a prosperous position. He did it by assuming complete responsibility for his results. He focused on changing the bad habit that had crept in and transformed his belief about himself to achieve the outrageous results he today enjoys.

One of the biggest keys to thinking big, thinking like a billionaire, is unwrapping the genius in you and understanding that you are the cause of your life, not the effect of it.

For instance, when Donald Trump walks down a street in New York City and looks at a building, he sees a potential investment. The vendor serving coffee on the street corner looks at the same building and sees only the corner where he can set up his kiosk. Here is entrepreneurship at its best. They are both businessmen, but the difference is that one is thinking in terms of a multi-million dollar investment from which thousands of tenants will pay him residual income over the next decade or more. The other one is thinking in terms of how much the passer-by will pay.

Who will get the bigger results? It must be the one who expanded his thinking to include greater possibilities.

Don't get me wrong. Both are winning ideas; both situations will generate a healthy cash flow. But Donald Trump exercises his thought process through the unwrapped genius in him—the billionaire's way of thinking! Most people do not think that way and are walking around in trances of disempowerment, taking what they get, rather than what their hearts truly desire.

Let's take a good look at some empowering qualities of a billionaire:

Billionaires start small—They desire to be exceptional so they start small and keep at it. Most billionaires started from humble beginnings and did not emerge as overnight billionaires. Sir Richard Branson started out by publishing a monthly university magazine. Bill Gates' success came from his garage, and Dr. Andre Robert became a success story by cleaning bathrooms in a church.

They think big—They see the end from the beginning as they unwrap the geniuses in themselves. They refuse to allow their creative imaginations to be hindered by race, age, background, or fear. Their big dreams become their focuses, and they work toward those dreams and making them reality.

Warren Buffett said, "I knew I was going to be rich. I don't think I ever doubted it for a minute." Billionaires think big and develop the habit of big thinking. Nothing will convince them otherwise.

They are competitive—They become brutal and fight back if challenged. Most billionaires are competitive and thrive in a competitive environment. They believe that competition brings the best out in them—the unwrapped geniuses in them. They are focused and driven by passion. Take a look at billionaires, and you will observe they're focused in their dealings. They don't try to do many things at once; they focus on one thing. Bill Gates focused on software, and Michael Dell focused on computers.

Billionaires are goal setters—They spend time setting goals that are high and challenging, yet realistic and attainable. They do not renege on them until achieved. They believe they must have goals and purpose in their lives. If you do not have a goal, how can you measure your achievements and success? Take up the challenge, and think about that!

They thrive on criticism—Billionaires do not get absorbed by criticism. Instead, they get inspired by it. They welcome criticism since they see it as feedback to improve themselves. It may even thrill them as it enhances their signatures.

They have strong, self-imposed standards and believe in themselves—Billionaires take charge of their destinies and do not leave them to fate. Fate by no means is faith since faith, in itself, is believing to achieve the end from the beginning. Billionaires are strong-willed individuals with tough self-imposed standards. They do not compromise their standards because they know they can achieve them.

They have sheer persistence and total commitment—They believe that when the going gets tough, the tough get going. They press on even in the face of hardship. In actual fact, in times of hardship, they get even tougher. Despite acquiring tremendous wealth, billionaires remain committed to their calls and are not afraid even to make 180-degree turns, refocus, and achieve what they intended.

They learn quickly from mistakes and thrive on pressure—To billionaires, mistakes are lessons learned and areas of adjustment. They are human, and their mistakes can also lead to failure. However, they do not bow their heads in defeat. Instead they get inspired by failure and use it as a stepping stone to success. Billionaires thrive on tension and uncertainty. When Bill Gates dropped out of school, he had no guarantees, but look what he has achieved and the success he has had. Billionaires' minds immediately drift from chaos into saving the projects and press through with confidence and expectations of victory.

They have high levels of self-confidence and take carefully calculated, moderate risks—Billionaires very seldom make decisions on impulse. They research the facts and weigh up the return on investment. These facts will determine the levels of risk they are prepared to take.

They are opportunists and use money as the score—They are problem solvers looking out for opportunities to solve a problem and save the day. Billionaires move in when other people are moving out as they see opportunities before others. They will always attempt to turn problems into value and believe they can create value out of nothing.

This is an amazing statement: Billionaires are driven by passion and not money. They use money acquired from their businesses to move on to other business challenges. Billionaires use money as a means to keep score and are therefore not driven by the quest to make money. You must know you are a billionaire with a mindset like that!

They manage debt to their advantages—Debt is a double-edged sword that can make or break people. Billionaires have mastered the art of debt leveraging. While others stay away from debt, billionaires use debt as financial leverage to get richer. This is an art worth observing and cultivating.

> Financial leverage is the advantage the rich have
> over the poor and middle class.
>
> —RICH DAD (FROM THE BOOK,
> RICH DAD, POOR DAD)

If you are currently not getting the results you want in any area of your life or business, start by taking responsibility for your results. Expand what you believe is possible, and be on the "cause" side, not the "because" side of success.

Richard Branson, it is said, was born with unique talents like a great golfer or talented author. But Branson, along with many billionaires, had a record of mistakes and inaccurate risk calculations. However, billionaires have an extraordinary uniqueness bred in them, and that is that quitting is not an option. It's all about how quickly they recover from the mistakes made!

Billionaires are driven by opportunities and taking calculated risks. They are completely aware of their emotions and acknowledge them for what they are. With knowledge, understanding, and wisdom, they calculate the risks with caution. They carefully analyze the situation knowing their own abilities and limitations. They know they are taking risks and work hard to open new doors and eliminate short term thinking and limitations by keeping the long term goals in front of them. Should they err, they don't weep over what might have been.

Gamblers, on the other hand, jump into action. Rather than pay attention to overruling emotions, they often risk more than they can afford to lose. Then the snowball effect occurs as they take increasingly bigger gambles in the hope of covering up losses. A valuable statement to remember is, as the billionaires say, "Do not take risks on something you cannot control and fully understand."

Summary

We all have the same ability to break through the outer and inner barriers that sabotage our success and process of thinking as a billionaire. After all, it's only a habit away! In this chapter you have been given reliable facts on how to build and develop the characteristics and mindset of a billionaire.

Red Flag

Many entrepreneurs will not take the extra effort to understand the basic requirements and habits of a billionaire's mindset.

Words of Wisdom

To acquire wisdom is to love oneself; people who cherish understanding will prosper.

—PROVERBS 19:8

Journal

Billionaires have a minimum of 12 unique characteristics. Align your character (SWOT analysis) done in chapter 1, and record what habits you have to change in order to think like a billionaire.

Ask and Answer

Does my billionaire mindset accommodate my unique talents, giftings, and ideas, or do I have to make adjustments to my situations?

The list of my newly acquired billionaire habits: _____

_____

_____

My winning idea:_____

_____

_____

Am I a calculated risk taker or a gambler; why? _____

_____

_____

Chapter 5

INHERITED ENTREPRENEURIAL RESOURCES

The thing that stayed with me about my father is that whatever he was doing—whether it was a new venture in business or just the everyday operation of the businesses—he was always a hands on person. He left nothing to chance but was there to start the work day and to batten down the hatches at the end of each day. This attribute in his life built faithfulness within the ranks of the working staff because each business and project was guided by Dad.

I remember hearing the alarm clock going off at midnight, and he would go to the fuel stations he owned to collect the cash from the register and the attendants seven nights a week. When he failed to do this it was amazing how much went missing. Dad would spend hours building his stock-car for the racing circuit in Zambia, and some of the mechanics would stay over to help him and be part of his dream.

I recall as well the year Dad and my dear brother John flew to Frankfurt, Germany, to collect his new Mercedes Benz 450 SLC. He had a flair and a zest for life that was able to direct all his abilities and resources with such precision that it drew the attention of others—like metal to a magnet.

These abilities and resources that he taught us children by his own life's example gave me the edge to start my publishing business. I knew I could accomplish anything I set my heart and mind on because of the I CAN attitude my father deposited within me. I published and distributed fifteen *Golf* magazines (newsletter format) each month with the same hands on attitude Dad had shown.

I sold advertising for the magazines, did individual interviews for articles, and contracted many global personalities for the covers of my magazines. Here I was utilizing my internal resources into yet another diverse business arena.

During this very busy time of life, I began to train my daughter Renee, at the age of thirteen, to set up my appointments. Renee did so well she began to make calls for debt collection and began to grow in confidence and experience. Today she is a very successful businesswomen herself with unique marketing and sales skills.

That which my father had deposited into my life I was automatically planting into my daughter's life, empowering her to excel in the business of life.

Life is a business. It's time to appropriate and take advantage of your entrepreneurial resources for this great race of life. Tunnel your inherited entrepreneurial resources by doing anything and everything to move the venture forward, further and faster with the least risk. Bootstrapping, or channeling the genius in you, is a process all entrepreneurs should understand and nourish in starting and even maintaining a successful business. The conserving of financial resources to the extreme comes by doing most of the needed tasks yourself. In maintaining a successful business, bootstrap yourself and your management, and empower your staff. Do what you have to do to get your business up and running!

Mustering your needed resources can make a huge difference between success and failure, and many entrepreneurs fail to see this and squander their financial resources by employing and contracting unnecessarily. This is evident in statistics claiming that most new businesses do not last longer than four years. And that is even if they get past the first year! I personally believe it is because they take their eyes off the ball, lose sight of the end from the beginning, and become reckless.

Interestingly, in *Webster's Collegiate Dictionary*, one of the meanings given to resources is "an available means afforded by the mind or one's personal capabilities." In a nutshell, be passionate, resourceful, and wise to see your dream come true. With this, you will be leaving a legacy for generations.

The dilemma a majority of entrepreneurs are in is they need a vast array of resources but are habitually strapped for cash. This is true everywhere in the world. The common belief is that entrepreneurship is an easy alternative to working for someone, but the successful entrepreneurs know better and could spend hours telling their stories of endurance and tested faith. A word of advice as we journey through these chapters—make absolutely certain you know what it takes to be a successful entrepreneur. By the end of this book, you will be more informed on how to determine if you have what it takes to be an entrepreneur, captivate your dream, and turn it into a success to be enjoyed.

A gifted and determined entrepreneur is unstoppable and will not let the lack of money stop or slow him or her down. (We addressed this in chapter 2.) As a basic approach to resource mobilization and management, successful entrepreneurs seek to:

- Understand the role and sacrifices of an entrepreneur.
- Bootstrap to conserve financial resources.
- Do much themselves before employing un-

necessarily.

- Negotiate and barter for everything they need—a skill to develop.
- Oblige in using other people's resources.
- Obtain free resources whenever possible.
- Control resources rather than own them— outsource jobs.
- Borrow, rent, or lease.
- Maintain flexibility so that they are not locked into physical assets that become anchors (e.g. long-term contracts).
- Use copious amounts of imagination and be street smart.

Entrepreneurial resources fall into seven categories: product or service, people, logistics, finances, knowledge, infrastructure, and imagination. These resources need to be mobilized—time- lined to ensure everything happens at the right time at the right place with the right people. Put your entrepreneurial hat on, and let's go for it.

Product or Service:

You need to know with clarity exactly what your product or service is and the uniqueness you are offering to the customer. To be a "me too" product is not going to do it for you. Take some time and effort to research your unique selling point (USP). Speak to friends, family, and especially to a mentor or coach to guide you to present a document that proves the uniqueness of your product or service.

This is your starting point. Have a product or service that is needed in the marketplace. Remember to study your competitors, and never say you do not have any competitors—that belief is only coming from a position of denial, not strength.

People Resources:

The ultimate resource for your venture is YOU. Entrepreneurs often neglect themselves in the intensity of the entrepreneurial voyage. Pay attention to your personal, emotional, and physical needs. Ensure you are spending quality time with family and friends and in leisure time for yourself. Burnout is not an answer!

The following resources require in-depth wisdom when making appointments. Gather and study information in detail to make the correct decisions:

- Partners
- Management team
- Company culture
- Advisors
- Business service providers
- Family and friends

Physical Resources:

A guiding principle in entrepreneurship is to control rather than to own physical resources. Real estate, equipment, machinery, and manufacturing and research facilities are physical resources—very capital-intensive ones at that. Risk is reduced by using physical resources that belong to other companies.

Identify and research the physical resources your product or service will require. Once you have identified the relevant needs, it is easier to then contact and meet with like-minded, related service providers and negotiate from a position of strength because you will have clarity and confidence in your negotiations.

Financial Resources:

This is probably the most comprehensive document you will ever prepare as an entrepreneur: the financial resources. We will address this in more detail in chapters 7, 8 and 12.

From the day you commit to building your business, you are destined to be absorbed in mobilizing, allocating, controlling, and generating this most crucial resource. Your venture will need money at every stage of its evolution, from start-up to maturity. If your business is doing well, you will need working capital for growth. If your business is in trouble, you will need money to regroup and restructure.

Many entrepreneurs never think about a funding plan, yet it is absolutely crucial to the success of the business. Money is the fuel needed to get your venture onto the runway. If there is no fuel—money—you cannot take off. You need money to develop, market, and test your new product or service, to purchase inventory, to pay for the first several months of office rent, to buy equipment, and to pay salaries until cash starts rolling in.

Here is a funding plan with six elements which will get you thinking about how to structure your specific financial needs:

- Clarify your business goals.
- Understand your money needs at each stage of your business plan and growth.
- Select appropriate sources of capital (second job, etc.).
- Improve your chances of equity investor interest—percentage ownership.
- Take the most likely path to early-stage funding—quickened funding.
- Orchestrate the funding process—list funding targets and the preparation for these meetings.

Knowledge Resources:

Knowledge resources encompass many topics: patents, proprietary know-how, research and development capabilities, access to contract researchers, outsourcing, access to licensable technology, and creative ways to employ existing technology to give you an edge.

Your competitors cannot easily reproduce the proprietary know-how that makes your business special. If yours is a service business, clients hire you because you understand how to do something that they do not know how to do; this is your unique selling point (USP).

Infrastructure Resources:

Productivity, efficiency, professionalism, and profits suffer without effective infrastructure. It is important to have up-to-date computer networks, software programs, social networking, information technology, communication systems, wireless capabilities, operating manuals, quality control procedures, underlying support systems, etc. This varies from business to business and must be integrated in the business plan as a high priority.

Imagination Resources:

Your imagination is your power tool. No other tool can move you faster or further. Let your imagination out of the box, and spend time brainstorming your business. Create channels to success that may lead you to:

- Unique access points into the marketplace.
- Distribution channels never thought of.
- Complimentary international markets
- Brand connections into new markets.
- Opening of doors to people and places of all kinds.
- Strategic partners.
- Key customers.
- Key suppliers.
- Service providers—marketing, advertising, subcontractors.
- Core competencies of all kinds—negotiators, strategic business planners and directors, the CEO's position.

Mobilize Your Resources:

You need to prepare a timeline milestone chart. This chart will be incorporated to direct and mobilize your daily action steps. You will notice when you start preparing your timeline milestone chart that there may be tasks that overlap. However, each detailed list of specific resources will be captured accurately on the chart, so all follows orderly and nothing is left to chance.

Summary

Mobilizing resources should be one of the first things you think of as you pursue your entrepreneurial goal. The genius in you will highlight crucial areas as you prepare your business plan in detail.

Red Flag

An entrepreneur thinks money is just going to flow in without any form of planning to raise money for the project.

Words of Wisdom

> Discretion is a life-giving fountain to those who possess it, but discipline is wasted on fools.
>
> —PROVERBS 20:22

Journal

1.) Develop an action plan to mobilize needed resources. Check the seven categories.

2.) Don't be constrained by what you own. Plan: What? When? How?

3.) Set time aside to have a brainstorm on imagination resources. Let your imagination take you to places, people, and means you have never been.

Write down all these channels your imagination has taken you to.

Ask and Answer

What is stopping me from starting my business plan at this very minute? Activate the genius in you right now!

List my newly acquired channels of business to be added to my business plan:

_____

_____

List the sources of capital and their requirements: _____

_____

Example of a Timeline:

Project Management Funding Success

MON	TUES	WED	THUR	FRI	SAT

Make list potentials					
	Contact list for appointments				
	Prepare forecast, collate references, business plan, legal docs				
Make list of appointments			Prepare presentation		
Continue making appointments					

Once the amount has been identified and recorded plan the funding process:

1) Make a list of potential funding resources.

2) Prepare detailed contact list of whom will be contacted for an appointment.

3) Make the necessary appoints to meet with the potential investors.

4) Prepare a professional presentation.

5) Prepare financial and forecasts of projected income and expenses and banking details.

6) Prepare and collate letters of reference.

7) Check and insert your business plan.

8) Prepare and present relevant legal documents.

Chapter 6

DO NOT MESS WITH ME!

A round the world, the challenges of life greatly affect people in all walks of life. The continent of Africa is no different than any other continent or country. Northern Rhodesia was changing, much of Central Africa had, becoming the nation of Zambia, and with it, came a struggle for power in the government. Life on planet Earth was about to change for our family. Many of my family were entrenched in businesses, farming, and even the school systems, but change was rapidly arriving.

Government curfews were imposed across the country, and we had to be home from work or school by 5 p.m. and inside our houses from 6 p.m. until 6 a.m.. Because of the lawlessness across the nation, we had to have security guards with guns to guard the house and properties. We children understood the gravity of this situation from very young ages.

Life's challenges happen all the time, and that is why we call it life, but it is how one handles these challenges and situations that produces winners out of losing situations.

Literally thousands of people were caught in these situations across much of Africa, caught up with a government change which led to tribal conflict and much blood shed.

Dad had raised us young children to have responsibility, to work, and to develop our skills in many areas of business life and life on the farm with our grandparents. He was a great sportsman which encouraged us in many and varied sports and exposed us to opportunities. We were ready for what we were about to be thrust into.

The tenacity I have today I got from my father. I not only worked with him but was trained by him to handle the pitfalls of life and bounce back. I know inside of you is a plan for your life, and I am here to help you to bring the treasure inside of you out to be presented to the world.

You are the future, so get your act together and work in your genius. Reach for your predestined future. Remember it is your gifting that you identified in chapter 1. You can do it, the billionaires did, and we know it's only a habit to be cultivated!

To cultivate a new habit takes quite a dose of will power. The problem isn't really setting new habits; it is, however, our approach to the subject that matters. Many people have experienced over and over again that their will power dwindles after a few days or a few weeks. Let me assure you, it's not their will power but their approach and attitude in setting a new habit that is working against their natural ways. Drastic steps, from one extreme to another, are where the real problem lies, and that is what makes it difficult.

Let's review. Gather your notes, and look at your unique gifting, your signature idea, and your billionaire principles. Remember the "I can" attitude to plan the winning formula and to enforce and maintain your new habit. To be a successful entrepreneur with a unique and brilliant idea, one must stay motivated, absorb information, strategize, and plan a financial breakthrough that will elevate your business concept into billionaire status.

We need to move out of the theatrical stage and into reality by working in our conscious minds of power and clarity. May I just mention this? You should remember that there is a transition period as with anything in life! A good example would be taking a trip/holiday. You would prepare and make decisions regarding the traveling details. Not so? You don't just get into your car and start driving.

Beginning a totally new thing may be a shock to your mind, body, and soul. So, one step at a time in the right direction is the correct approach. This new way is not yet a habit but an intrusion to the mind, and your mind may not be sure how to deal with it making things seemingly worse. Old habits die hard, so be strong in developing your new billionaire status.

Here are some easy ways to activate your new habits during reading and applying entrepreneurship to unwrap the genius in you:

- Know what you want clearly and write it down.
- Make a list of benefits of your new habit.
- Plan step for step how you are going to enforce that habit daily.
- Set goals to be reached at each step and your rewards in achieving such.
- Go for consistency. Believe me, this is key!
- Find yourself a mentor to quicken the process by keeping you on track.
- Commit to the process of the new habit.
- Remember that quitting is not an option; it's a poor choice.
- You will unwrap the genius in you. It's just a habit, my friend.

Another interesting subject to deal with, which is very prevalent in our society today, is the blame game. Research has shown that an organization or group with a culture of blame has a serious disadvantage when it comes to creativity, learning, innovation, and productive risk-taking. The virus that spreads is the habit of protecting one's self-image. The blame game is huge globally as people do not want to be held accountable and do not want to look like fools in the information era. Therefore, mistakes are hidden or people pretend to know. (How sad.)

A committed entrepreneur has the gifting of discernment and empowering people rather than dwelling on their mistakes. There are times when people's mistakes will surface in public but can be addressed without publicly humiliating them. The following guidelines may alert your senses to the blame game:

- Don't blame others for your mistakes; you will help prevent a culture of emerging blame.
- When confronting others, do so constructively; preferably doing so in private and not lashing out in public.
- Always focus on lesson learned; develop an attitude of learning.
- Blame always betrays in the end; own up and be a hero.

The best years of your life are the ones in which you decide your problems are your own. You do not blame them on your mother, the economy, or the president. You realize that you control your own destiny, and by lying and blaming others you are basically quitting on your own destiny. The fact is, every one of us works around day-to-day chaos and frustration, and we all go through complex and desperate situations of some sort or another. It is in how we deal with it that will bring us joy and peace and make everything worthwhile in the end.

Life isn't fair, and we do not get to choose every circumstance, but we do get to make the correct choices and work with the decisions we make. Entrepreneurs have the unique quality of solving problems and look at obstacles as opportunities to strengthen their characters in problem solving and help themselves and others with minimum effort.

You could be sabotaging your relationships with unnecessary "emotional baggage." Don't spend time thinking of it, but rather get rid of "emotional baggage" as it hinders your future success. You have one life, your life, and you spend every hour in it, so make a choice with me in the following pages. The truths I share with you are going to change your life for the better for generations to come.

Where does "emotional baggage" come from? Let's explore a few areas.

Tragic Loss:

You may have experienced an irreplaceable loss of safety in your living situation, self-confidence in your abilities, a parent or family member's courage to take additional risks, self-respect in order to expect respect from others, or trust in someone. Within this frame, baggage is the scar from a deep loss.

Someone Else's Baggage:

You may have taken the brunt of other people's acting out, going ballistic, losing their grip, displacing their anxiety, misdirecting their self-contempt, or some other form of abuse. You may feel trapped by their aggression or challenged to fight back with an alarmed sense of chronic danger. We react with our survival instincts.

Drawing a Blank:

Others may have silenced your unique voice, the display of your feelings, or unconventional point of view. We acquire repressive baggage from getting told to stop what we're thinking, feeling or expressing.

Our baggage keeps us stifled, inhibited, or blocked from realizing our hidden talents and extraordinary gifts and valuable character traits.

Sabotage Attempts:

We may find our baggage taking control of episodes in our lives repeatedly in business success, personal relationships, or new projects at home. Our baggage may contain a belief system about our dreadful destiny, cruel fate, or perpetual bad luck.

Being Patient With Our Shortcomings:

Emotional baggage can make us very difficult to get along with. When acting like jerks, whiners, control freaks, bigots, or downers, our baggage is running our show!

Pretending To Have No Baggage:

We pretend or masquerade that we are in control of our lives. We keep up the illusions of being civilized, rational, thoughtful, and respectful of others.

Hasty Decision Making:

We continually live with the consequences of having been so wrong, vulnerable, foolish, unguarded, or trusting at the moment when the decision was made. No one can tell us any differently, and our decisions stand unchallenged.

Here two unique pointers to look out for in situations:

Projecting Self-Doubt:

- This is a crucial behavior that needs to be worked on because it shows the worst in yourself. You see the reflection of yourself in others, and you start to make assumptions about them that are very dangerous.

Becoming Paranoid:

- In order for relationships to work, you have to trust others. One's paranoia can manifest itself in some extremely unattractive ways: neediness, dishonesty, suspicion, clinginess, and breach of privacy.

Summary

This has been a rather heavy chapter, but we need to be fully prepared to launch into our new journey. Entrepreneurship ... unwrap the genius in you!

Red Flag

Not many people will take the time to do self-evaluation and record it. They will carry baggage for decades unable to release the geniuses in themselves.

Words of Wisdom

> Get all the advice and instructions you can, and
> be wise the rest of your life.
>
> —PROVERBS 19:20

Journal

1.) Write down the three new habits you want to develop and the reasons for wanting to do so.

2.) Write down three reasons how your baggage can subconsciously encourage you to play the blame game.

Ask and Answer

What will the rewards be should I work through these two questions with due diligence and accuracy?

YOU ARE A HIGH ACHIEVER; YOU HAVE PROVEN THAT BY WORKING THROUGH THESE VERY IMPORTANT QUESTIONS AND ANSWERING WITH FRANKNESS:

My attitude adjustment to make: _____

_____

My number one new habit: _____

My two reasons for not taking baggage into my future: _____

Chapter 7

MONEY RULES

In the beginning, business can be tough if it is cash flow stricken. There are always options available. However, considerable research and calculation must be completed before decisions are made. There are many options, and caution must be taken to avoid incorrect decisions that could exert a poor influence on your business success.

After being in business for approximately eight years, I hit my first cash flow problem. It was due to me not following the game plan. I had extended to my customers debt repayment terms. This was a difficult time for me. I didn't know the best way to handle my collections department because Dad never got himself into that position. This was a lesson I had to learn and quickly—otherwise, I could have lost it all.

Dad could have helped, but I wanted to figure it out myself. I began the investigation and the researching of different options with banks and potential investors. Both were self-driven and required a majority share in my business. Soon, I came across a factoring business which, for a small fee, would purchase these debts each month on the condition that I would supply them with all the sales contracts' details monthly. They would invoice the customers and ensure all funds were collected. This arrangement came with their guarantee to recoup the majority of their funding. The system worked well, and within four months, my cash flow was in a healthy position again.

My situation improved drastically when sales increased, debtors paid punctually, and a good cash flow was maintained. With a healthy cash situation, one operates from a position of power, strength, and wisdom, and opportunities seem to be attracted by the confidence one portrays in the business arena.

Money rules; there is no doubt about that. Many lessons were learned during that season of my life. In hind side, it taught me a great deal about the management of the finances and the importance of cash flow. It was exceptionally restrictive to be without money in the bank; credit cards became my means of survival. Believe me, they are such a waste of money.

Attracting other confident business owners is exactly what happened to me when my finances were balanced. Here's what happened when I joined a golf club in Cape Town and learned to play a good game of golf (off a twelve handicap). I met Ernie Els, the famous South African golfer on the pro circuit. After meeting, Ernie contracted with me to launch his golf magazine *Something Else*. I had positioned myself to be strong and visible in the business world and was now reaping the benefits. (In *Something Else*, I published Ernie's achievements and those of gifted boys and girls he teaches through his golf academy.)

It is important to understand the rules of money and how it can work for you, but it takes time, sacrifice and endurance.

Opportunities come in all shapes and sizes. True wealth is recognizing opportunities when they come. Many people often mislabel profitable opportunities as problems. If opportunities don't come often enough, we must have insight on how to spot them and pursue them until we achieve success. It is essential that we learn to see the wealth of opportunities all around us.

Remember the program *Who Wants to Be a Millionaire?* This became a popular catch phrase throughout the world. Let's face it; all of the fixation on shows about money, getting rich, stock market millionaires, and huge lottery payouts leads to the question, "Who doesn't want to be a millionaire?"

Everyone has concerns about money: debt, mortgage, investments, cash flow. Everyone thinks about how it is related to daily life and business success. We need to make our money work for us so that we don't spend our lives working for it. We need to increase our financial educations. I will share some interesting financial statements made by some of the wealthiest people in the world.

Be Humble:

> When you do not know a thing, allow that you do not know--this is knowledge and brilliance at its best.
>
> —MARIETTE KUSSMAUL

> Being humble in the face of uncertainty keeps you from costly mistakes. You won't jump on yesterday's bandwagon. And before you invest, you'll be more likely to ask a key question: "What if I am wrong?"
>
> —JASON ZWEIG

Investing is a big bet on an unknowable future. The mark of wisdom is accepting just how unknown it is. Granted, that is not easy. Our brains are built to think the future will be like the near past. We're too ready to act on the predictions of pundits (learned persons, experts, or authorities) who are no more clued in than we are about what lies ahead.

Have An Emergency Fund:

> For age and want, save while you may; no morning sun lasts a whole day.
>
> —BENJAMIN FRANKLIN

The first step in constructing any serious financial plan is to create an emergency cash fund. This is, ideally, three to six months' living expenses stashed in a low-cost ultra-safe bank account or money-market fund. Without this financial cushion, any unexpected expense can derail your long-term plans.

Mix It Up:

> It is part of a wise man to keep himself today for tomorrow and not to venture all his eggs in one basket.
>
> —MIGUEL DE CERVANTES

Nothing can break the law of risk and reward, but a diversified portfolio can bend it. When you spread your money properly among different asset types, a rise in some will offset a fall in others, muting your overall risk without a commensurate drop in returns. It's the closest thing to a free lunch there is in investing.

Average Is The New Best:

> The best way to own common stocks is through an index fund.
>
> —WARREN BUFFETT

Here's the logic behind index funds which aim simply to match the return of a market index. The average fund in any market will always earn that market's return because aggregate investors are the market, minus expenses. Since index funds match the market but have much smaller expenses than other funds, they will always beat the average fund in the long run. It's hard to argue with the math, and history bears it out.

Be Thrifty:

> Performance comes and goes, but cost rolls on forever.
>
> —JACK BOGLE

If you choose a fund that eats up 1.5 percent a year in expenses over one that costs 1 percent, let alone the 0.2 percent that index funds may charge, your funds return will have to beat the other's by half a point a year just for you to come out even. Past returns are no guarantee of the future, but today's low-cost funds are likely to stay low cost.

Buy Low:

> If a business is worth a dollar, and I can buy it for forty cents, something good may happen to me.
>
> —WARREN BUFFETT

The best Dow stock of the past has been Caterpillar (CAT). It made the cut with a 212 return. In 1997, in the midst of tech madness, the market was so bored by the company's industrial-machinery business that investors paid just $11.50 for each dollar of earnings. If the stock's current value of 16.1 times earning is right, then that's nearly a 30 percent discount. Smart investors didn't need to foresee the coming construction boom. They only needed to call a bargain a bargain and trust the market to eventually wise up.

Borrow Responsibly:

> As life closes in on someone who has borrowed far too much money on the strength of far too little income, there are no fire escapes.
>
> —JOHN KENNETH GALBRAITH

Face the truth; if you let them, lenders are only too willing to advance you more than is good for your family. Mortgage banks and credit-card issuers don't care if your monthly payments make it impossible for you to sock money away. You need to set your own rules and standards.

> No credit cards—period. It's never okay to pay interest on what is borrowed for consumption.

Borrow only to buy assets that appreciate: a home, yes; an education, sure; a vacation, a fancy dinner, or even a fifty-inch flat-screen, not wise.

Talk to Your Spouse:

In every house of marriage, there's room for an interpreter.

—STANLEY KUNITZ

Your most important financial partner isn't your broker. It's your spouse—you know, the one who probably owns half of all you do and whose fate is inextricably linked with yours. However, research shows that spouses often don't agree on even such basic information as income and savings. This is a wake-up call. To make smart decisions, you need to talk, and if you're like most couples, you need to do a better job at it.

MEN: Don't assume she doesn't care about this stuff. She does, but you need to lay off the jargon and speak English.

WOMEN: Don't just leave it all to him. At a minimum, know where the key papers are and how your money is invested.

BOTH: Focus on goals, not on who's right. It's not a contest.

Give Wisely:

The time is always right to do the right thing.

—MARTIN LUTHER KING JR.

Granted, Dr. King did not have money on his mind when he spoke these words. But they also ring true in your financial life; giving back is always the right thing. Still, there are more right and less right ways to do it.

Look beyond the headlines. It's fine to give to relieve the effects of disasters like tsunamis, but don't forget about smaller charities that go wanting. Don't give over the phone. Telemarketers often take a cut of 50 percent or more. Focus. Identify a cause that really speaks to you. Then devote most of your energy and charitable dollars to the organizations that best support it.

Keep Money In Its Place:

> A wise man should have money in his head but not in his heart.

> —JONATHAN SWIFT

People who say they value money highly report that they are less happy in life than those who care more about love and friends. Enough said.

Summary

Here is my take. It's still a good investment to buy property:

- In good condition.
- Good location—Location is everything.
- The property must be an asset not a liability.
- Income generating.
- With sufficient parking.
- Buy at below market value.
- Develop the asset to increase property valuation to the national current market valuation.

As a back-up, keep a safe stocked with silver and gold (or other precious metals).

Red Flag

Many people never study the possibilities of where they should invest and which investments would give them the most reliable returns. They find themselves being reckless and impulsive. Where are you on this subject?

Words of Wisdom

> The wise are known for their understanding, and instruction is appreciated if it's well presented.

> —PROVERBS 16:23

Journal

List your available investment options. (how, where, and when)

Prepare your strategy on debt cancellation.

Ask and Answer

Where do you stand on the subject of investment and cash flow building?

Whose investment strategy made the most sense to you and why?

_____

_____

Write down the date on which you will be totally debt free:

_____

_____

Chapter 8

DISCOVER THE PLANNER INSIDE OF YOU

Millionaires and billionaires make tremendous sacrifices and choices. They recognize and effectually engage the planners inside of them. They have clarity in their thinking and confidently communicate who they are; these are simply practiced habits!

Planning is a talent that is almost forced upon us by necessity. It could be through sacrifices, problem solving, or just planning a good holiday for the family. Our lives' daily situations mandate that we make plans; that is, of course, if we value quality lives and would rather have fewer problems and more joys. Planning and structure guides us through chaos in a more focused and joyful manner eliminating unnecessary stress and wasted time.

By now, I am certain that you have come to the conclusion that my father is rather an interesting character with capabilities that can only have come from above. Surely he had times of trial, but it's how he adapted to them, how he approached them, and how he took steps to solve them.

Dad is now nearly eighty years old and still such a blessing to the family. Everyone knew that if one needed a word of wisdom—go to Dad, go to Neville Halberg. He will give the right advice. How does this happen? He understands the vital role of planning and approaches the situation with wisdom and clarity. He knows how to solve the problems and take the correct action.

There is a beautiful town on what is known as the Garden Route Coast of the Cape Province called Sedgefield, South Africa. It is considered to be one of the most beautiful spots in the world. Dad has his holiday house there. He loves the outdoors and loves cycling to the beach with his wife Erna. Recently, he found cycling rather difficult as he is getting on in years. Seeing his seeming limitation, he planned his solution and took appropriate action. He purchased a petrol powered motor for his bicycle, so that he can still cycle up those rather steep hills to the beach. He overcomes hindrances by planning. All things are possible—believe it.

My daughter Michelle is also a planner. When our grandchild Garron was born, Michelle made the decision to be a stay-at-home mom. Obtaining her desired goal required planning. Financially, it was tough for her, but the rewards have been great as she has gotten to spend many hours with her son lending personal guidance and support to his gifting of sports. She, too, has her own small business called Pet Sit Stay @ Home. She has structured the business around Garron's sports.

From generation to generation, the gift of entrepreneurship has been prevalent in my family. This book is possible due to my comprehension of the planner inside of me. My great grandparents were pioneers from Denmark and owned a butchery in South Africa. My grandparents grew maize and tobacco and raised cattle in Zambia and later in South Africa. My father, my genius example, applied his expertise of planning in all that he put his hand to: business, innovation, sports, and leisure. He excelled having discovered the planner inside of himself.

The planner is inside you. All you need to do is follow the exercises in each of the chapters of this book, and step-by-step, you will recognize you can do it. You will see the planner inside of you; work your plan!

Planning requires a number of steps to be taken. No journey of desired consequences begins without a plan. Planning is an intellectual exercise and a conscious determination of courses of action.

If you want to get where you intend to go, you need a road map, a GPS. Without it, the outcomes of all your labors will be random, disappointing, or devastating at times.

In this chapter, we will identify specific headings and topics with a short synopsis of what content should be written under each. You will be empowered to prepare and structure your complete business plan and discover there is a planner inside of you.

The body of your plan, approximately twenty-five to thirty pages, should discuss the following topics:

HEADING—TOPIC	DESCRIPTION
Executive summary: At least 4 pages:	Tell the story to yourself. Introduce your business idea. Summarize the points below in an interesting and convincing manner.
Owner profile:	Describe your experiences and passions in business and in life. Prepare your 30 second commercial.
Company description:	Detail what type of business it is—its vision and mission statement.

HEADING—TOPIC	DESCRIPTION
Product concept:	Define the essence of your product or service.
Industry dynamics:	What is happening in the industry and the size thereof?
Customer analysis:	Who are your customers, and what are their needs?
Competitor analysis:	Who are your competitors, and what slice of the pie do they have?
Strategy for gaining competitive advantages:	Identify your unique selling points (USP). Outline a promotions strategy.
Marketing and sales plan:	Prepare a comprehensive marketing plan. Forecast a sales plan.
Manufacturing and operations:	Determine your manufacturing strategy—owned plant or outsourced? Prepare a comprehensive project plan with resources allocated—include timelines.
Product development:	Illustrate a comprehensive plan to maintain a unique product to encourage new customers.

HEADING—TOPIC	DESCRIPTION
Management team:	Prepare job profiles. Prepare competency profiles. Present accountability trackers for managers. Identify "specific" character traits. Hire winners.
Business design:	Prepare an organic company structure chart.
Five-year financial structure plan:	Research similar companies for facts and figures. Some can be based on assumption.
Funding required:	Develop a funding needed plan. Identify specific "loaners" not scammers.
Funding allocation:	Prepare a project plan to allocate funding in the business and on the product or service.
Keys to success:	Record lessons learned to refer to in the future.
Red flag areas:	Prepare a red flag column on the right side of your plan and record possible problem areas to every part of the business plan.
Milestones and schedules:	Formulate schedules where required—timelines. Record milestones—5 years or 10 years later.

Here are a few critical planning steps for the serious entrepreneur to consider:

- Plan the future and set goals.
- Communicate directions, goals, and progress.
- Hire winners and game breakers.
- Get organized and set the example.
- Use critical path indicators (red flags).
- Track the course and adjust.
- Build trust through communication.
- Focus energy and don't get scrappy.
- Celebrate success.

Business owners, managers, and executives have to consider various courses of action, achieve the desired goals, and detail the outcomes of every course of action.

Planning Is Goal-Oriented:

Established goals should have general acceptance otherwise individual efforts and energies may be misguided and misdirected and will not achieve the desired results.

Planning Is Forward Thinking:

Planning requires thinking beyond the current situation or circumstance. It depends upon analyzing, researching, and preparing the desired outcome for a win-win situation.

Planning Contributes To Objectives:

It contributes positively to attaining the objectives of the business. These are, therefore, easily achieved.

Planning Is Sound Judgment:

Planning is a mental exercise involving creative thinking, sound judgment, and clarity of imagination.

Planning Involves Decision Making:

Managers are surrounded daily by a number of choices and alternatives. They have to make quality decisions based upon requirements and resources available to them.

Planning Is A Primary Function:

Planning lays foundations for other functions of management and specific deliverables.

Planning Encourages Innovation:

Planning encourages innovation and creative thinking among the managers and related staff as many new ideas come to the mind—brainstorming.

Planning Is A Daily Process:

Planning is a never-ending function due to the dynamics of the business environment. It is an invaluable trait to remain in the habit of planning.

Planning Is Designed For Efficiency:

Planning accomplishes and maintains the required objectives. It also anticipates unpredicted costs.

Planning Increases Competitive Strength:

Effective planning gives a competitive edge to the business, products, or service. It involves changes in capacity, methods, quality, fates, and fashions of people and technology.

Planning Is Flexible:

Under certain circumstances, the original plan of action should be revised and adapted to new trends that may present themselves.

Planning Evaluates Alternatives:

Having sought out the available alternatives along with their strengths and weaknesses, planners are then required to evaluate the alternatives giving due respect to various factors involved.

Planning Reduces the Cost of Performance:

It removes hesitancy, avoids crises and chaos, eliminates misdirected steps, and protects against misjudged deviations.

Derivative Plans:

Plans do not accomplish themselves, and they require supporting plans. (For example, a marketing plan is supported by a promotions plan.) These plans working together form the derivative plan. Keep in mind that communicating plans should also be shared with the organization. Communication is a key to working plans.

Executive Summary:

As you construct your executive summary, include only the essential topics. Investors scrutinize a deal based on its merits not its hype. The following ten points should assist you in preparing a solid and professional summary:

- The uniqueness of your idea.
- Owner profile and credibility of the team.
- Your business design, supporting operations, strategies, and revenue streams.
- The value adds for your customers.
- Company pricing strategy.
- The time and calculation of break-even sales.
- Sustainable competitive advantages.
- The marketing mix or market dynamics.
- Financial projections and forecasting.
- Red flag or key risk areas.

Summary

Discovering the planner inside of you is a big advantage. Consequently, you will be able to record accurately, clearly, and comprehensively your business plan with a sense of achievement and sheer joy.

Red Flag

As an entrepreneur, you need to pay attention to your executive summary's details and be as concise as possible. Banks determine their decisions based on executive summaries.

Words of Wisdom

A lazy person sleeps soundly and goes hungry.

—PROVERBS 20:20

Journal

Prepare your four-page executive summary.

Start preparing the first draft of your business plan.

Ask and Answer

Why is the executive summary so important in the business plan?

Do I have sufficient information to start the first draft of my business plan?

_____

_____

Do I have a mentor or coach who could read my draft business plan?

_____

_____

Chapter 9

BRANDING IS THE NAME

What we think of ourselves and how we portray who we are is a daily event in our lives. Circumstances affect us to a certain extent. However, each of us is like a brand. We invite people around us to either enjoy us or to avoid us.

Dad, himself, is a brand—a master innovator evident in his personal signature! His friends and the people around him were automatically attracted to him. He had oodles of confidence, was fun to be around, and had gifted business know how. The fact he knew that his many businesses were running efficiently and that he had a solid return on his efforts made him even more attractive. His brand attributes attracted like-minded people everywhere he was. These were the brand benefits Dad offered as a wealthy member in the team of millionaires and billionaires.

Every one of us represents our own brand: successful, secure, insecure, confident, humble, pleasant, unpleasant, etc. Your passion exuberantly attracts others into your arena as you are recognized as someone who may be rather interesting. Therein, your brand personality is revealed.

Approximately twenty-four years ago, I had the privilege of working with one of the most caring mayoresses, Trudy Williams, of Cape Town in South Africa. She, as all the mayoresses before, had to introduce a community project which would enhance the lifestyle of a particular group in the community. Trudy wanted to do something for the under-privileged children in Cross Roads, Cape Town, and with all in agreement, "Toys for Smiles" was launched.

The brand "Toys for Smiles" was a Christmas project inherited by mayoresses for the next decade. The logo, project slogan, national television and branded advertising campaign, promotional material, point of sale structures, distribution points, and school drives were the results of the brand strategy which was very important and ensured the success of the project. The community was encouraged to donate new and used toys at schools and selected retails stores. The mayoress, herself, was a brand personality who promoted the concept that it was a social responsibility of every individual who cared for children to donate a toy. "Toys for Smiles" was the benefit exchange of the brand. This was one of my "pet projects" as it was a joyful experience with cherished memories.

Branding is rather an interesting feature in the marketing mix which a majority of entrepreneurs neglect. Brand strategizing has an effective psychology which may challenge you to a new way of thinking about where you wish to position your company or products. Take up the challenge, and make your brand known and respected.

Brilliant brand names succeed because they are unique. They engage interest and stimulate conversation. They're not just names but platforms of success stories that support future company growth and product expansion. When a company gets it right, the brand's promise is reinforced, and brand equity and sales rise above its competitors—leveraging real business performance.

Every successful brand appeals both to the hearts and minds of potential customers; it is built around an irresistible idea. This idea has real value and meets the needs of customers, the organization, and its stakeholders alike.

Your brand may experience outrageous success due to its niche position in the marketplace and by its unique selling features. Therefore, you need to protect your brand by creating a brand manual. I advise you to engage a professional agency to assist with this manual.

A network of suppliers, advertisers, design agencies, photographers, printers, and marketing companies may be appointed to the task of executing the company's image. This includes your company's message and its core competencies on designated projects. Because they are not you, they may not fully understand your company's vision.

Therefore it is important to create your brand manual with clarity. This manual will smartly and officially ensure that the organization's members and associated outsourcing companies are all on common ground (the same page) regarding the following:

- Registration, copyright, and trademarks
- Logos
- Logo usage
- Corporate branding
- Product branding
- Colors
- Fonts
- Company stationery
- Company portfolio
- Images
- Advertisements
- Presentations
- Promotional material
- Television coverage
- Social networking
- Customer experience

Brand Manual: A Necessity

Many entrepreneurs have the view that it is not necessary for such a manual until a similar business is started down the road. Frankly, that's too late. Here are a couple of wise reasons why you need a brand manual:

- To remind the public that behind the brand is a company that invites trust, support, and confidence.
- To enhance marketing and sales efforts so that effective use of the brand logo, design, and expression generate a positive impact.
- Product branding goes beyond the product. It communicates what your company stands for.

Brand Manual Content

Without defining core guidelines, all channels of communication become hit and miss. Therefore, it is imperative you know the facts you want to publish.

Considering what it stands for, the brand's description should run parallel with the values of the company.

- Prepare a list of situations in which the brand and its symbols may and may not be used.
- Express the tone and use of words relating to the brand (e.g., slogans, etc.)
- Specify colors, dimensions, lines, accents, inclusions of trademark, brand signature, image styles, etc.
- Determine typographic style elements.
- Illustrate reproduction guidelines for advertising agencies and printers.
- Record the quality statement required for your brand.
- Stipulate your brand's promises.
- Demand consistency in the production of

the above specifications.

Your brand is not a name, logo, website, or advertising or public relations campaign. Those are only the tools—not the brand. A brand is a desirable idea manifested by your products, services, customer needs, and the experience of offers.

Brand Strategy

It is defining your brand strategy that allows you to incorporate marketing, advertising, public relations, and social media to consistently and accurately reinforce the character of your company. Focus on what you do best, and then communicate your inimitable strengths to your customers and the general public. Your brand is your business model which represents your mission and vision statements.

Create New or Refreshed Positioning
for a Company or Product

The six brand essence requirements are essential to launch or maintain a solid brand in the market place with its identified customers. It will be worth your time and effort to concentrate on and strategize each factor to strengthen your company and brand.

The Brand Essence

This is the heart and soul of the brand. It's a timeless quality that describes what it is.

Brand Vision and Culture

A brand, in order to be accepted and loved by customers, operates much like a culture. Everything the company does, every product or service it offers, every public statement, advertisement, website, social network, internal policy, and business decision must be aligned with its vision and mission statements.

The consumers must join the brand culture and participate in that culture as a way of expressing to the rest of the world they are believers of the brand.

Name and Logo

Early branding of a small or emerging company is essential to business success. It is the quickest way for your company to express what it is and what it can offer.

Inaccurate branding of a new business can make it difficult for people to grasp why the business even exists in the first place. This is very dangerous; it could cost you and defeat a good idea.

Brand Attributes

Brand attributes relate to its function or a unique feature. They are the benefits that are offered to the target market.

Brand Position

It defines everything your brand is to that specific target market (niche market) that fulfills its unique need.

Brand Personality

It is a comprehensive concept. (See the diagrams at the end of this chapter.) Brand personality includes the intangible traits of that brand: its beliefs, values, prejudices, features, interests, feelings, and heritage. Find what is unique about your brand. Study your target market, and join the two.

Brand Proposition

A good brand proposition must be simple and easy to understand. It is the promise that a brand makes. Therefore, it is critical that the brand's promise is easy to understand, consistent, engaging, unique, and relevant to the target audience. It should always address the audience's current needs and future aspirations.

A good brand proposition will be able to connect with its audience on an emotional level. It has been statistically recorded that a strong emotional connection can create valuable brand equity.

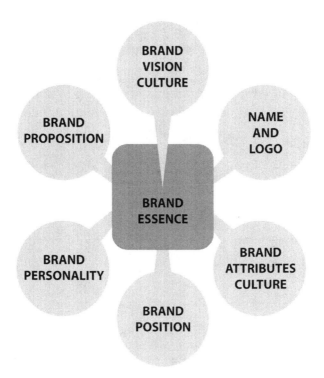

Summary

Branding communicates what your business is. It is the heart and soul of your core business and its products. Treat it with respect, and it will give you return on your investment.

Red Flag

It is important to think big and prepare yourself professionally for your future success. The brand manual is essential! Do not neglect this opportunity.

Words of Wisdom

A person's words can be life-giving waters; words of true wisdom are as refreshing as a bubbling brook.

—Proverbs 18:4

Journal

Prepare your brand manual by writing down what you want to incorporate in the manual. (See page one of this chapter for guidelines.)

Prepare your unique brand strategy referring to the "Brand Essence" diagram for assistance with the explanations of each topic.

Ask and Answer

Do you need to speak to a marketing expert to ensure you completely understand the value of brand strategy?

I need more information on:

_____

_____

My understanding of brand strategy is:

_____

_____

Chapter 10

CONFIDENCE PERSONIFIED

The constant example set before me was one of total confidence no matter what my father attempted whether a new business venture or sport activity. In everything he participated, he always did his best. This confidence, which Dad carried within himself, was contagious and drew me into the same flow with my own life and future. There was an exacting precision in all the achievements he accomplished, and this trait took root in my life.

Dad became the president of the Rotary Club in South Africa. This club had the biggest events and raised the most money for the projects they did. With this great example in my life, doors of opportunity were very obvious to me, and I grew to automatically think, I can do that. I continue to live from this position of confidence in all the affairs of life.

When Richard Branson introduced his IMAX theatre into Cape Town, I worked with him and his team in the launch of the project. There is something about working with billionaires that allows a person to see into the ways they think. I came to the realization of what Dad had prepared me for in my early years. It was the confidence to be able to work side by side with billionaires and on assignments like the IMAX project.

This particular project added to my insight and understanding of what a person like Richard Branson was seeing, thinking, and executing. I identified the same attributes encouraged in me when I was around twelve years old. The same projecting of confidence, needing and requiring precision in every area of the IMAX launch, and never taking anything for granted was taught by Mr. Branson.

I lectured for the Dale Carnegie courses. As I taught, each concept and principle took root within my heart and mind. In the teaching of this lecture series to many people, I benefited greatly from this knowledge. As a result, yet another layer of wisdom was deposited in me stimulating the writing and publishing of this book!

Each of these accumulated layers of knowledge and wisdom have continued to build my confidence to work with and advise directors and CEO's of major companies in Africa and other countries. I have been empowered to lead the staffs and managements of many different companies because of this layer of confidence my father and others placed within me.

You ask, "Was it easy?" No, easy does not live with excellence. It was hard, and there were times of pressure which only caused me to reach deep inside myself to find the hidden answers and develop the needed strengths for the impossible to be possible. Thanks, Dad, for your wonderful example.

First, let's take a look at the definition of confidence. *Confidence*: belief in the powers, trustworthiness, or reliability of a person or thing; belief in oneself and one's gifting and abilities, or certitudes; assurance about success.

As a global traveler, I wish to share the three most important gifts you have which should enable you to network from a position of confidence. People are drawn to confident people; there is just something intriguing about them. Confident individuals stand out in a room full of people and invite masses into their areas comfortably changing the atmospheres around them and sharing themselves with each and every person present!

Confidence does not happen overnight; it is developed by becoming aware of our attitudes and changing our habits. It's simple, but commitment is required. To be confident on a daily basis, it takes time and effort to practice this desired habit. It has been documented by specialists that it takes twenty-one days to develop a new habit. Make the decision. Let's start day one!

Habit One:

A Warm Personality Makes Me Approachable

Research has shown touching something warm can make you feel and act more warmly toward others. Yale University scientists researched to determine if physical warmth could promote psychological warmth, and subconsciously prime people to think better of others. They recruited 41 college students for what the students thought was personality research. A lab worker escorted each participant up the elevator of Yale's psychology building and casually asked for help holding her cup of coffee, either hot or iced, while she recorded the student's name on a clipboard.

Inside the lab, the students were given a description of a fictitious person described as industrious, cautious, and determined. They then rated that person's presumed personality traits. Students who had held the hot cup saw the person as more generous, sociable, and good-natured than those who had held the cold cup. Yet, there were no differences between the two groups on ratings of honesty, attractiveness, or strength—traits not associated with either warm or cold personalities.

Then these researchers recruited 53 different students for a second study. The students were to briefly hold heat or ice packs (those sold in drugstores for pain) allegedly as part of product testing. In fact, the test was to find out which items the students would choose as "thank you" gifts for participating: ice-cream coupons or bottled drinks for themselves or for friends.

Students who held hot packs were more likely to choose rewards for friends, while those who held ice packs were more likely to choose rewards for themselves.

The conclusion to be drawn from this episode is that very subtle cues from the environment can significantly influence behavior and feelings. Other research has found that the same brain region that processes physical temperature changes, called *insula,* also processes feelings of trust and empathy associated with social warmth. I said all of this to get to this point: A confident person with a warm personality is like a hot chocolate with a dash of whip cream and marshmallows on a cold day. You can feel the warmth of confident people as they make you feel welcome and wanted.

Develop the habit of being a warm, confident person and training your personality to be pure and uncompromising:

- Be sincerely interested in what people are saying.
- Genuinely be thankful for what they are doing.
- Put them first.
- Be warm and kindhearted.
- Be non-judgmental, and speak from a heart of goodness.
- Share experiences and knowledge.
- Be satisfied with who you are, and listen to others.
- Do not exploit others' kindness and help.

Habit Two:

Integrity Rules the Mind to Riches

When we pander for approval from others and trade our values and beliefs for it, we will suffer the consequences. Seeking what others have will be costly. You need to know what it will cost you and if it is worth it to have what they have. Will I renounce my integrity in the process?

Integrity means to be who you are and not try to be someone else or something else! It is to be true to oneself and one's values, beliefs, and standards. It also means not to fall into some unethical ways to achieve success.

Whatever we want to attain, we must let go of the lesser in order to obtain the greater. Every goal requires sacrifice of some sort but not that of one's integrity. Old habits of thinking and behaving prevent us from manifesting our desires and goals. Listen to this: There is no way we can continue to behave as victims and also become victorious.

Giving others permission to determine what you think, feel, say, and do means you will become as they are. Once you recognize how others manipulate you by stipulating your future through their words and actions, you will operate from a position of strength and make progress. By allowing this kind of manipulation, your personal integrity is being compromised!

Integrity is doing something right, for the right reasons, without harming others while doing it. It is goodness of the purest form. Integrity is held at the highest level of esteem in business and should never be compromised. Owning integrity will release confidence in others who do business with you.

Concentrate on these lessons to develop a wholesome level of integrity:

- Be yourself; do not pretend to be something you are not. It will be obvious to others if you are fake.
- Do not compromise your integrity for anything in the world.
- Understand there will be sacrifices to uphold your integrity.
- You have integrity; therefore, you are a victor and not a victim.

- Do not be manipulated by your circumstances.
- Do what is right for the right reasons.
- Integrity will be the foundation as your confidence grows.

Habit Three:

Self-Education as an Entrepreneur

Self-education increases confidence and success. There is no better way to open your mind to opportunities and develop wisdom than to educate yourself in areas lacking. As an entrepreneur, you need to have an excessive base of sound knowledge and understanding of how to run a business. The bonus is your confidence grows, and you become a genius of habit.

Benjamin Franklin decided to improve his writing abilities while he apprenticed at his brother's printing shop. He created a number of methods designed to make him a better writer by studying the writings of authors whose style he liked and practicing writing essays in the same style. He would also rewrite essays by famous writers and seek to improve them. Another method he devised was writing the paragraphs and sentences of an essay on slips of paper, shuffling the slips, and attempting to reassemble them in the correct order.

Also during his apprenticeship, Franklin was exposed to a variety of books and read everything that he could get his hands on. Not only was Franklin an avid reader, but he loved to discuss what he read—just as entrepreneurs do.

One of the reasons Franklin formed the Junto in 1727 was to have a ready forum in which to explore and discuss intellectual topics. He identified his gifting, his niche, and with great passion, he pursued it with diligence. The members of Junto sought to improve their minds and their world. They helped one another in business and found ways to help others in their community. Brilliant entrepreneurs, they worked in their genius.

Six Positive Attitudes Toward Self-Help:

- Persistently empower your mind to achieve continued success in reaching your billionaire status.
- Acknowledge who you are, and accept your faults; more importantly, emphasize your abilities.
- Do the things you enjoy doing, and learn to explore new opportunities.
- Do not try and change yourself to please others but rather to build your riches.
- To obtain success in both your personal life and as an entrepreneur, you need to study the composites of personality types.
- Continually identify your areas of weakness as an entrepreneur, and prepare a structured plan of action to further your education and maintain a successful legacy for generations.

Summary

I leave you with this inspiring quotation from Ralph Waldo Emerson: "The man of genius inspires us with a boundless confidence in our own power."

Red Flag

Many entrepreneurs do not take the time to educate themselves but believe they will learn as they go along!

Words of Wisdom

From a wise mind comes wise speech; the words of the wise are persuasive.

—PROVERBS 16:23

Journal

Record which of the three habits you really need to concentrate on and perfect.

Which areas of self-help do you need to work on?

Ask and Answer

Do I compromise my integrity? If so, what must I do to stop this habit immediately?

My personality traits:

_____

_____

Changes to make to my personality in order to have a warm confident personality:

_____

_____

Chapter II

BEWARE OF PITFALLS

For a few years, I found myself running around like a headless chicken. I had too much to do and too little time in which to do it. It seemed that my deadlines were never met but rather carried over to the next day. My thoughts went back to the years spent with my father; I was amazed at how much he managed to get into his days: running all his businesses, meeting people, participating in sports, racing cars, and providing for the family.

I made a decision: I was going to start training for the Comrades, an ultra-marathon. The course was between Durban and Pietermaritzburg. (Durban is located in Kwa Zulu Natal, South Africa.) This race was unique in that one year it was an "up" race from Durban to Pietermaritzburg, and the following year it was a "down" race from Pietermaritzburg to Durban. I had the privilege of running it both ways.

The Comrades was an ultra-distance equivalent to sixty-three miles with a cut-off time of eleven hours. Because of certain pre-race qualifications, I trained approximately three hours every single day. This consisted of at least two thirteen mile races, two twenty-six mile races, and one ultra-distance race of forty miles. All had to be achieved within two months of the Comrades. To train correctly for ultra-marathons, take a good two years with complete commitment. Approximately five thousand runners would participate, so the race was pretty popular among the runners internationally.

Training for this race taught me many lessons as time went on, and, by default in some cases, I had to make adjustments to my lifestyle: changing eating habits, sleeping longer hours, and enduring all weather conditions. My social life became non-existent as I was always training or running marathons to qualify. Apart from the hours of running, there were also many hours in the gym spent using machines for strength and core stability training. These disciplines were physical aspects of the training in developing endurance for the many hours on the road. However, this was the easy stuff, especially when one gets a second wind, and it feels as if one could run forever and ever!

The battle was more in the mind; the body was mostly willing, but the mind struggled as it had never had to stay focused for so many hours. The first five hours were managed without too much discipline. It only really began after forty miles when fatigue would settle in, and the mind was not too willing to continue. It took intense discipline to take control of my thought process from the negative and keep it positive and willing. Self-talk had to stay positive, songs were sung, and the support of other runners was much appreciated.

Discipline is something that must be cultivated and maintained in order for a person to become a true entrepreneur. Success has its sacrifices as ultra-marathons do; patience and long hours of planning and strategizing are necessary to achieve the ultimate success. Business does not just happen and can become very difficult at times. Your self-talk, mentor, family and friends will be your anchors, so keep them close.

When you start a new business, the last thing you want to focus on is failure. The successful entrepreneur is that man or woman who inwardly has a hunch, a knowing, an instinct, and a unique and tangible project. However, if you address the common reasons for failure up front, you'll be much less likely to fall victim to them. You have already established your strengths and weaknesses in chapter one and have identified your passion-driven gifting in chapter two. You are working on your billionaire mindset and are utilizing your inherited entrepreneurial resources to program your success as an entrepreneur in a time such as this.

In this chapter, we will be addressing pitfalls. There are key factors that, if not avoided, may decrease the longevity of your business. Pay careful attention to the nudging of your inner spirit — your gut. Then engage in intelligent, proactive risk taking. There is always a calculated risk in starting a new business and during the longevity of your business.

Beware of the Well

You could either drop the bucket in the pit or pull in buckets of overflow in your new business venture. It all depends on your decision making supported by research and wisdom from above.

Pitfall Number One

No mentor. Having a mentor empowers you with extra eyes, ears, and valuable wisdom and encouragement. This person should be older than you and passionately understand the responsibilities of an entrepreneur as well as understand your endurance and uniqueness.

Mentors should encourage you in a variety of areas:

- Expertise and wisdom—They have knowledge and expertise. They have been there and know when to say, "Have you thought of this possibility..."
- Confident networking—Mentors are established professionals. Once you start working

99

with a mentor, you can tap into that person's network of contacts.

- A big picture view—Your mentor will contribute a fresh view point. You may be so focused on your business plan or your next contract that it can be difficult to see your business in the long term.
- Confidence building—Mentors help you refine your vision and make certain you're on the right path to achieve success.

Pitfall Number Two

Fear of failure. Fear can alert you to red flags. However, fear is overcome by gathering the truth of the situation through information and research. Consider your status to be powerful; you have almost completed this book. You have also recorded your every intuition in preparing yourself and your business plan as a successful entrepreneur with confidence and purpose. Fear handicaps confidence.

Pitfall Number Three

Lack of knowledge of the marketplace. Research, research, and again, research. This is the key factor in gathering information to make absolutely certain you understand everything that is happening in the marketplace where you will be positioning your brand, your product, and your company. We addressed this in Chapters 5 and 9. You know who you are and who your target market is and how they move in this market.

Pitfall Number Four

Poor management. This is rated in the top three reasons for a business to fail; that's how serious it is. Insufficient understanding of the complete structure of your business equals poor management. The complete structure of your business includes finances, purchasing, sales and marketing, production, hiring skilled staff, brand strategy, communication, planning, vision, and leadership.

A passionate entrepreneur is skilled at strategic thinking, able to make his vision a reality and to encourage his team to participate in this reality while confronting change, making transitions, and preparing for new possibilities in the future.

Pitfall Number Five

Inadequate financial planning. We will be addressing how to prepare a financial plan in the next chapter, and I believe you'll grasp a few new tools. It is imperative you calculate how much money your business will require, not only for the start-up costs but the costs of staying in business.

Summary

There are, of course, other reasons for failure in business. Ultimately, make sure you are in business for the right reasons. Otherwise, you may find yourself saying, "I wish I'd never started this venture," and it may become obvious that it is too late!

Red Flag

Remember to checklist your possible pitfalls throughout your business plan.

Words of Wisdom

It is better to be patient than powerful; it is better
to have self-control than to conquer a city.

—PROVERBS 16:32

Journal

List your areas of possible pitfalls. Do you have a trusted mentor?

Ask and Answer

Ask yourself and your mentor, "Am I starting up a new venture for the right reasons and not for just making money?"

My one personal pitfall:

Chapter 12

DEVELOP WISDOM IN YOUR FINANCES

The term wisdom is amazingly profound and Biblical. King Solomon is known to have been the wisest man on planet Earth. I firmly believe that wisdom is entrenched in us through enduring the lessons of life and business ventures.

My father was a man of wisdom; he achieved so much during his lifetime. I am certain many lessons were learned as he developed his entrepreneurial gifting and blessings to share with his family and his friends. He spoke with confidence; he shared his experiences on the "how to" with conviction. He probably faced most of the challenges relevant to the questions he asked himself.

Before Donald Trump, Robert Kiyosaki, or Richard Branson, there was Neville Halberg from Africa leading the pack in wisdom. This wisdom began when he was small and living in a third world country. He was a mentor to many other wise men, millionaires and billionaires, farmers, business entrepreneurs, the police force in Zambia, and his family and friends alike. He never withheld information; rather, he sought to share wisdom, lifting others to their maximum capabilities.

Cash flow was king in Dad's businesses and received much of his time in preparing and planning for a new business venture. He understood the importance of cash flow, the inward and outward balances of keeping money moving. Timely investments were sensitively managed as he made certain there were adequate free and liquid finances. His focus was building healthy returns to prevent himself from taking costly loans.

The great entrepreneurs of the Industrial Age were a diverse lot. First and foremost, as they ventured, took calculated risks, and looked at the world around them, they saw possibilities where others saw problems and pitfalls. They took the risks necessary to develop new products, new services, and new ways of doing business. Like entrepreneurs today, they ventured into an environment of revolutionary technological and economic change. Dad's philosophies were challenged when Dr. Kenneth Kaunda became President of Zambia (1964) and again during Fredrick Chiluba's rise to power (1991). He fought his way through the nationalization of businesses, the repossession of farmland by the government, the education system falling apart, and the food crises the country has had to endure even to this day.

Henry Ford said, "My advice to young men is to be ready to revise any system, scrap any methods, and abandon theory if the success of the job requires it." Well, Dad understood this statement; he had to practice it given the challenges he and the family had to endure in Zambia—a country he loved and protected as a reserve policeman in the police force. He was passionate about recreating that which had been destroyed and proved beyond a shadow of a doubt he was not going to subject himself to a dictatorship he did not believe in.

I firmly believe I'm a chip off the old block. Like Dad, I have a zest for life and a passion for business which captivates my every thought process and desire.

I also love to share my new ventures with like-minded people and to mentor them through the processes of achieving their dreams and accepting the genius in them.

To God be the glory!

> In my young manhood, we had everything to do and nothing to do it with; we had to hew our own paths along new lines; we had little experience to go on. Capital was most difficult to get, credits were mysterious things.
>
> —JOHN D. ROCKEFELLER

In preparing the business plan, there is a tendency to adorn the financial estimates with impractical figures and poorly conducted market research. This is not wisdom but rather foolishness as no business will ever succeed on adorned estimates and assumptions. This is a fact. Business owners need to understand that a financial plan takes a considerable amount of time to create. Any figures provided in the plan should be practical and supported by proper market research demonstrating how those projections were calculated. It is advisable to hire a skilled professional who can tailor the financial plan more accurately to its field of projections and accountancy.

In my years of entrepreneurship mentoring, I have been absolutely shocked at the percentage of people and business owners who do not know how to read financial statements. Believe me, if you can read a nutrition label, you can learn to read a basic financial statement. If you can follow a recipe or apply for a loan, you can learn basic accounting. You, as a business owner, have inherited entrepreneurial resources and can easily understand your financial statements.

In this final chapter, you will grasp an understanding of how your business is doing financially and how to predict and plan for the future. A sound understanding of financial statements will help you:

- Increase your confidence when talking about money and finances.
- Identify unfavorable trends in your business operations.
- Monitor your cash flow requirements in a timely manner.
- Monitor periodic increases and decreases in your wealth.
- Monitor your performance against your financial plan.

Bank Statements

A bank statement is going to list all the withdrawals and deposits that have been made in a month's time. Also found on the bank statement will be checks (although not necessarily in order), electronic transfers, and debit card purchases. All transactions will be recorded, and you can request a bank statement whenever you require one from you bank.

Income Statement Or Profit And Loss Statement

An income statement is a report that shows how much revenue a company earned over a specific period. It also reveals the costs and expenses associated with the earning of that revenue. The literal bottom line of the statement shows the company's net earnings or losses. Now you know how much the company earned or lost over the period.

Income statements also report earnings per share (EPS). This calculation indicates how much money shareholders would receive if the company decided to distribute all of the net earnings for the period.

Shareholder's Equity or Capital or Net Worth

This is the money that would be left if a company sold all of its assets and paid off all of its liabilities. This leftover money belongs to the shareholders or the owners of the company. A company's assets have to equal the sum of its liabilities and shareholders' equity.

Statement of Changes In Owner's Equity

This statement is used to bridge the gap between the amount of owner's equity at the beginning of the period and the amount of that equity at the end of the period.

The Balance Sheet

It is a statement of the company's relative wealth or financial position, assets, and liabilities at any given point.

Cash Flow Statements

These statements report a company's inflows and outflows of cash. These are important because a company needs to have enough cash on hand to pay its expenses and purchase assets. While an income statement can tell you whether a company made a profit, a cash flow statement can tell you whether the company generated cash. Cash is always king in a business!

Cash flow statements record the information from a company's balance sheet and income statement. The bottom line of this statement shows the net increase or decrease in cash for the period. Generally, cash flow statements are divided into three main sections: operating activities, investing activities, and financing activities. With a new business venture, it also includes the start-up activities (not many companies do this).

Know the difference between start-up costs and operating costs:

Start-up costs:

- Any fees that can be applied prior to the launch of a company and the period of time during the early stages of a company's development.

Operating costs:

- Any expenses associated with sustaining the company throughout its development and longevity.

The Management's Discussion and Analysis

You can find a narrative explanation of a company's financial performance in a section of the quarterly or annual report entitled Management's Discussion and Analysis. MD&A is management's opportunity to provide investors with its view of the financial performance and condition of the company. It's also management's opportunity to tell investors what the financial statements show and do not show, as well as important trends and risks that have shaped the past or are reasonably likely to shape the company's future.

Financial Statement Ratios and Calculations

It is interesting to know these phrases: "P/E ratio", "current ratio", and "operating margins." What do these terms mean, and why are they not revealed on the financial statements? There are only a few ratios that investors calculate from information presented on financial statements and use to evaluate a company:

- Debt-to-Equity ratio—Compares a company's total debt to shareholders' equity found on the company's balance sheet. Debt-to-Equity ratio = total liabilities/shareholders' equity.
- Inventory turnover ratio—Compares a company's cost of sales on its income statement with its average inventory balance for the period.
- Operating margin—Compares a company's operating income to net revenues. (This is also found on the income statement.)

No one financial statement tells the complete story. However, combined, they provide very powerful information for the owner/s or investors. Information is the investor's best tool when it comes to investing wisely.

Forecasting and prediction is another financial skill required by an entrepreneur. This strategy is incorporated when sales forecasts have to be recorded in the sales and marketing plan which in turn assists with budgeting. Forecasting is objective, scientific, reproducible, and free from bias. Error analysis is possible in it. Prediction, however, is subjective, mostly intuitive, non-reproducible, and individual biased. Only limited error analysis is possible in predictions.

The table difference between forecasting and prediction:

FORECASTING		PREDICTION	
1	Involves the projection of the past into the future.	1	Involves judgment in management after taking all available information into account.
2	Involves estimating the level of demand of a product on the basis of factors that generate the demand in past months.	2	Involves the anticipated changes of the future. It may include even new factors that may affect future demand.
3	Is more scientific.	3	Is more intuitive.
4	Is relatively free from personal bias.	4	Is more governed by personal bias and preference.
5	Is more objective.	5	Is more subjective.
6	Is generally referred to as "Throw Ahead" technique.	6	Is generally referred to as "Saying Beforehand" technique.
7	Error analysis is possible.	7	Does not contain error analysis.

FORECASTING		PREDICTION	
8	Is reproducible. (The same result would be obtained every time using any particular technique.)	8	Is not reproducible.

Summary

Financial statements are intricate and essential to a business plan. It is not a business plan until you are able to understand and record your financial situation in a convincing manner to yourself and your investors.

To conclude the final pages of this book, I'm going to share one last nugget with you—much like the strawberry on the top of a delicious dessert.

The Feasibility Study

Truly, this is the cherry on top. Everything you have read, journaled, and planned can be confirmed as being a viable option for you the entrepreneur ... the unwrapped genius in you! A feasibility study looks at the viability of an idea with an emphasis on identifying potential problems and attempts to answer one main question: Will my idea work, and should I proceed with it?

Have you identified correctly how, where, and to whom you intend to sell your product or service? Have you made certain that you have assessed your competitors correctly?

Feasibility studies address issues such as where and how the business will operate. These studies provide in-depth details about the business to determine its success and serve as valuable tools for developing a winning business plan. Each step of your business plan can go under the feasibility microscope.

Why are feasibility studies so important? The information you gather and present in your feasibility study will help you:

- List in detail all the things you need to make the business a success.
- Identify logistical and other business-related problems and solutions.
- Develop marketing strategies to convince a bank or investor that your business is worth considering as an investment.

Service is a solid foundation for developing the final draft of your business plan.

Components of a Feasibility Study:

- Description of the business—Details the product or services to be offered and how they will be delivered.
- Marketing Feasibility—Includes a description of the industry, current market, anticipated future market potential, competition, sales projections, potential buyers, etc.
- Technical Feasibility—Details how you will deliver a product or service (materials, labor, transportation, location of business, technology required, etc.)
- Financial Feasibility—Projects how much start-up capital is required for the project.
- Organizational Feasibility—Defines the legal and corporate structure of the business.
- Conclusion—Discusses how the business can succeed. Be honest in your assessment because investors won't just look at your conclusions; they will also look at the data and will question your statements if they are unrealistic.

Red Flag

Do not think you know it all. Study financial documents to empower yourself.

Words of Wisdom

> The Lord despises double standards; he is not pleased by dishonest scales.
>
> —PROVERBS 20:23

Journal

Write a note to yourself to include the financial documents you need to spend time on to confidently understand them.

Prepare a feasibility checklist of all plans, forecasts, resources, etc., that need to be qualified through a feasibility study.

Ask and Answer

Does my mentor say I am ready to launch?

You are now an entrepreneur ... the genius is unwrapped! You have everything clearly planned and strategized, your mindset is in the right place, your idea is unique, you understand your customers' needs, your management structure is in place, you have inherited resources, your brand solid and funding structure is inviting, your financial report projects steady return on investment, and your dream is ready to be released.

I trust you have enjoyed this book as much as I have enjoyed writing it and found it to be of help in preparing your business plan and strategizing your future as an entrepreneur and a new world expert.

So what are you waiting for? Go get it. You are a genius!

REFERENCES

www.trump.com

www.freefamousquotes.net

www.henryfordquotes.com

www.minterest.com

www.johnkennethgalbraith.com

www.brainyquotes.com

www.thinkexist..com/quotes/john_d._rockefeller

New Living Application Study Bible (The Book of Proverbs)

ABOUT THE AUTHOR

Mariette Elizabeth Kussmaul is a highly motivated person with strong business skills and a passion to see projects through to completion. Her unique ability in the area of business strategy and forward thinking is a beneficial quality as she strives for excellence in all she undertakes.

She has a sparkle in her eye that few people have; a born entrepreneur. Her skills extend to facilitating workshops and training at a high level of proficiency creating excellent levels of motivation and ownership in others.

Her sensitivity to identify problem areas in the workplace is a gifting that supersedes any situation requiring a unique solution. This gifting is sought after by many CEO's as they engage her in their business environment to highlight areas of "turbulence" resolving the situation and projecting a profitable scenario.

Mariette is a strong teacher and has the ability to energize and lead others as they study or work with her. She is self motivated, a spontaneous communicator, as a co-host with her husband, Ronald, on their television show Point Destiny. She has the ability to teach and reach viewers with a high degree of retention in their lives.

Point Destiny reaches millions of people throughout the world on TBN Africa.

CONTACT THE AUTHOR

Market Place Motivations LLC

Mariette Elizabeth Kussmaul

Website: *www.marketplacemotivations.com*

Tel: (208) 321 1274

Fax: (208) 321 1278

Email: *mariette@marketplacemotivations.com*